SCOTLAND'S CRUEL SEA

Also by Robert Jeffrey

Peterhead – the inside story of Scotland's toughest prison
Gentle Johnny Ramensky
The Barlinnie Story
A Boxing Dynasty (*with Tommy Gilmour*)
Real Hard Cases (*with Les Brown*)
Glasgow's Godfather
Gangs of Glasgow (*first published as* Glasgow Gangland)
Glasgow's Hard Men
Blood on the Streets
The Wee Book of Glasgow
The Wee Book of the Clyde
*

Clydeside People and Places
The Herald Book of the Clyde
Doon the Water
Scotland's Sporting Heroes
Images of Glasgow
(*All with Ian Watson*)

SCOTLAND'S CRUEL SEA

*Heroism and Disaster
off the Scottish Coast*

Robert Jeffrey

BLACK & WHITE PUBLISHING

First published 2014
by Black & White Publishing Ltd
29 Ocean Drive, Edinburgh EH6 6JL

1 3 5 7 9 10 8 6 4 2   14 15 16 17

ISBN   978 1 84502 886 2

A CIP catalogue record for this book is available from the British Library.

Typeset by RefineCatch Limited, Bungay, Suffolk
Printed and bound by Gutenberg Press, Malta

CONTENTS

ACKNOWLEDGEMENTS

Tom Bone, Ray Bulloch, Ronnie Brownie, Ian Bruce, Jim Campbell, Jamie Campbell, Paul Drury, David Frost, Dr Grant Jeffrey, Dr John Riddell, Anne Riddell, John Linklater, Forbes Ferguson, Freddie Gillies, Stuart Fyfe, Dr Stuart Jeffrey, Stuart Irvine, Sylvia Irvine, Nelson Norman, Bill Pye, Ronald Ross, Tommy Ralston, John Steele, Noreen Steele and the staff of the Mitchell Library, Glasgow.

This book is dedicated to the memory of those, famous and unknown, who died in Scotland's cruel sea. And those who tried to save them.

INTRODUCTION

There are few more pleasant ways to pass a summer afternoon than to stroll along a deserted beach or walk a seaside cliff path. Scotland's rugged coastline has plenty of both, be it vast sweeps of glittering sand such as Sandwood Bay in remote Sutherland or the north-east cliffs of Buchan and Fife. You could have that stroll many miles from the nearest town or village. Or you could be on the doorstep of either of the country's two largest cities. No matter – if you gaze out to sea, in summer calm or winter gale, you are probably looking at the site of a shipwreck. Beneath our seas lie around 5,000 known wrecks, with countless others yet to be discovered.

A 'shipwreck map' – produced in the spring of 2014 by the Royal Commission on the Ancient and Historical Monuments of Scotland and Historic Scotland – dramatically illustrates the toll taken by Scotland's cruel sea. The map is part of a necessary long-term project by marine archaeologists which aims to protect our underwater heritage from damage by offshore wind turbines or tidal energy projects.

As marine archaeologist George Geddes remarks: 'The map helps us understand what might be lost if wreck sites are disturbed. We don't want to destroy a potential *Mary Rose*.' Its value to the nation's heritage apart, the map reveals the problem of a writer faced with telling the tales of tragedies in our seas – he or she is spoiled for choice. No matter how much research and work goes into the project, only a fraction of the dramas can be told. There are no rules on what should go in and what should be left aside. This book is not intended to be definitive or comprehensive. The choice of the stops on a journey round Scotland's dramatic coastline is idiosyncratic. However, those with an interest in maritime matters will have a shipwreck tale or tragedy of special interest. If yours is not in this book, I apologise. Perhaps it could be told in another volume!

Robert Jeffrey

Cumbernauld was a place where those decanted from the inner city could take a lonely wander around featureless housing estates then largely devoid of the cosy, if deprived, companionship available in even the worst slums of Gorbals and Brigton. Many writers ignore the horrors of outside toilets, substandard housing and the volume of crime and wickedness that were a feature of these slums known worldwide. Rose-tinted spectacles were in demand as some scribes looked back on the old days in Glasgow's deprived neighbourhoods. However, Cumbernauld may have provided better housing, but it could be the joyless sort of place memorably described by one Scots comic as a 'desert with windaes'.

However, the strong local spirit of Brigton infused the thousands who gathered in Shawfield Stadium to watch Clyde on the day of this disaster. But any optimism on the terraces about a pleasant afternoon of football was, as the match progressed, cruelly dismissed. At the game I was in the company of my father, who, perhaps with a nod in the direction of his Brigton relatives, was a fervent supporter – or at least as fervent as a highly intelligent, well-rounded and laid-back man could be – of the 'Bully Wee', as Clyde were known. For him it was a home match; for me an away game, as I was a follower of the now defunct Third Lanark, who played in Cathkin Park, a couple of miles away from Shawfield. The fact that when Clyde were playing away, Thirds would be at home and vice versa meant we could go to each ground on alternate Saturdays. No family feuding! I remember nothing of the game itself, but one incident is never to be forgotten. It was announced over the public address system that there had been a disaster in the Irish Sea that stormy afternoon. There was no detail – it was far too early in the story – but the Brigton Irish knew full well that relatives and friends could be in trouble and many left the ground to seek further news. Football was of no importance after that. More than a hundred people lost their lives when the *Princess Victoria* went down.

When it went into service, from its home port of Stranraer, with London, Midland and Scottish (LMS) railway in 1947, the ferry was at the cutting edge of maritime technology. Although operated by the railway company, the vessel was owned by the British Transport Commission and was the first purpose-built roll-on roll-off ferry of its kind to serve in British coastal waters. Its route was from Stranraer to Larne for Belfast. The concept of cars and freight lorries simply driving on and off ferries through gigantic stern doors into huge, echoing and often foul-smelling holds is now commonplace. These days this method of loading is used worldwide in the ferry business and is even in use in fast catamarans as well as large ships, with car decks of several storeys.

Few remember or look back with any affection on the slow progress of loading in the days when cars were hoisted on cranes and dropped onto the open decks of ships. Roll-on roll-off is, in the modern idiom, a no-brainer. It was the future of car ferries.

The *Princess Victoria* was Clyde-built at one of the most famous and most innovative yards in the world: Denny Brothers in Dumbarton. As well as being involved in building some of the most famous ships in the world, including the *Cutty Sark* and the American river boat *Delta Queen*, this remarkable firm was also a pioneer of hovercraft and was even involved in flying boats for a short time. So when the *Princess Victoria,* or Yard Number 1399, was launched on

27 August 1946, it immediately became part of Scottish maritime history.

There had been four previous ships of the same name and her immediate predecessor had been sunk by a German mine in the Humber during the Second World War. On the day of the launch the usual champagne corks were popped and management, workers and their families toasted a bright future for this new maritime development, the roll-on roll-off ferry. Any launch on the Clyde is a happy, optimistic event; even today, when most of the tonnage gliding down the greased slipways belongs to warships, there is something of a party atmosphere. You never forget the sight and sounds of your first launch and the years of work that have produced an impressive ship, so its first taste of the water is something special.

So, as the *Princess Victoria* slid down the slips, leaving a murky trail of flotsam bobbing behind it, there was no thought that it would all end in black tragedy. The ship itself was 309 feet long, beam 48 feet and draught an impressive 17 feet. It was driven by two Sulzer diesels, which could push it to a regular 19 knots (around 22 mph). It could carry 1,500 passengers, 70 tons of cargo, forty-nine cars and had sleeping accommodation for fifty-four. But its most impressive and innovative features were the massive stern doors that would be the key to its demise.

But, for now, in its early years of service, the ship was a considerable success. An initial problem whereby, in certain sea conditions the gigantic stern doors needed assistance to keep water completely off the car deck, led to modifications being made and additional stern protection was lowered over the original doors when required.

The huge swells of the Irish Sea in a gale were to be a

problem. On the morning of the disaster, the ferry left Stranraer railway pier at 7.45 a.m. with 44 tons of cargo, 128 passengers and fifty-one crew members. There was a gale warning in force, but the commanding officer Captain James Ferguson, something of an Irish Sea veteran, with seventeen years of experience on the route, decided nonetheless to cast off. It may be unfair to suggest that perhaps there was a sniff of overconfidence in that decision, but it is interesting to note that current ferry practice, as followed by firms such as Caledonian MacBrayne, insists that skippers rotate ferries and routes regularly to avoid the possibility of overconfidence and complacency.

No matter his motives, the captain, who went down with his ship – some reports had him on the bridge saluting as his vessel slipped beneath the waves – and his crew demonstrated extreme bravery in the emergency. And the skipper was not to know that the stern doors were not to be up to the job that day. He also fought tenaciously to save the ship, and it is pertinent to remember that that weekend saw perhaps the worst gales of the last century sweep the British Isles and hundreds died in storm-related accidents up and down the country. The winds were said to have reached 100 mph. Weather forecasting, of course, was not at its current level of sophistication.

Another factor in the decision to sail was that from Stranraer there was a longish haul down the relatively sheltered waters of Loch Ryan. This meant that the crew had no immediate picture of the wild conditions to face them when they entered the open sea. But it seems from the start that spray was breaking over the ship, including the stern doors. This was significant and the new 'guillotine' style door intended for extra protection had not been lowered.

The problem was that putting the extra protection in place was cumbersome, labour-intensive and time-consuming. So, it was not much used. That helpful agent hindsight, however, suggests that if ever the extra protection was needed, it was on such a day as this.

Immediately outside Loch Ryan things began to happen frighteningly fast, and even the most experienced of travellers on the route were aware this was going to be no easy voyage. When the ship finally faced the full fury of the storm, a huge wave damaged the lower part of the stern door and the first of the water that was eventually to sink the ship got onto the car deck. The crew struggled manfully to fully close the stern doors, but the damage caused by the huge wave made it impossible, despite all their efforts on the heaving stern section of the now fatally damaged ship.

Had the 'guillotine' been in place, would this have happened? Again, with the help of hindsight the answer is probably not. The fact was that water was getting onto the car deck. In the normal run of events such water would simply wash away through the scuppers. This was not happening, probably because the leak was just too big. The court of inquiry into the accident highlighted design faults in the arrangements to get rid of water in these circumstances. As the crew fought to get the water off the car deck and prevent more coming in, the ship began to list disturbingly to starboard.

There are conflicting reports about quite when the rogue wave that caused the worst damage struck. Some commentators have it that it happened when the ship was still heading to Ireland; others say it happened after the decision to try to run back to the safety of Loch Ryan had been taken. Indeed, the whole saga of the sinking is riddled with question marks and conflicting accounts. Even in dispute is the exact number of those who died and an accurate account of the numbers on board. However, the most generally accepted figure is that 179 people were on board and only forty-four survived. It may be worth pointing out here that none of the ship's officers survived, unlike some more recent liner and ferry tragedies where on one occasion the Italian master was accused of being among the first off the stricken vessel. In another recent accident, the captain was said not even to have been on the bridge.

More than half a century ago, record keeping was not at the level it is now in the computer age. Undisputed, however, is the fact that events had swiftly got out of control. In the midst of all the drama, any notion Captain Ferguson had that the ship could be brought back under normal control vanished. He decided that a retreat into the more sheltered waters of Loch Ryan would be wise. To do this he intended to go astern, to steer the vessel with the bow rudder. It seemed a good idea. But there was further complication – hard as they fought in the wind and the wild spray, the crew could not release a pin that secured the bow rudder. Why is not clear, but perhaps poor maintenance or storm damage could have come into play. The brave efforts of the skipper and the crew could not be faulted, but the fact remains that the bow rudder could not be used in this emergency.

With escape to the shelter of Loch Ryan denied to him, Captain Ferguson had few alternatives. The one he chose was to run for the shelter of Northern Ireland itself, using a course that would hopefully keep the worst of the weather from further damaging his ship. Just what was going on in the minds of the poor passengers is almost too frightful to imagine. They were in deep peril on the sea and they knew it. After years of trouble-free runs between Scotland and Ireland, few saw any danger in the short trip. Suddenly all that had changed.

At 9.46 a.m., just two hours out from the safety of Stranraer, the ferry's radio officer, David Broadfoot, a man who was to emerge as a hero of the tragedy, sent his first message in Morse code, alerting the maritime authorities to the possibility of real disaster. It might sound odd now but back then *Princess Victoria* did not have a radio-telephone. But that hypnotic tapping sound of the Morse keys, familiar from countless war and disaster-at-sea movies, spelled out a chilling message: 'Hove-to off Loch Ryan, vessel not under command, urgent assistance of tugs required.'

By now the cargo was beginning to move and water was still coming aboard. Inevitably the list got worse by the minute. Forty-five minutes or so after that first dramatic plea for help, an SOS transmission was made. This was now a full-scale disaster.

At this stage the ferry was still heading towards Ireland, though at a mere 5 knots or so, and the huge storm of wind, snow and rain was still raging. The list caused by shipping water through the stern doors and the failure of it to clear away led to serious cargo movement, which exacerbated the list and was to cause problems with launching the lifeboats in the final moments of the ferry's life. Eventually water got into the engine room and there was then no hope.

The upgrade of the Mayday transmissions to a full SOS led to frantic activity on both sides of the Irish Sea. And in the skies above. As pointed out already, that weekend was the worst for weather in the last hundred years or so. Seafarers and their passengers were in trouble all round

Britain and the west coast of Scotland was particularly badly hit. Clearly it was, to say the least, not good flying weather, and as the *Princess Victoria* was fighting for her life, further north the RAF had deployed a Hastings aircraft into stormy skies to assist rescues off Lewis and Barra. Eventually the plane was redirected south towards Ireland and arrived at the disaster area after the ferry had sunk. Nonetheless, the aircrew were able to drop supplies and assist in guiding HMS *Contest* to the scene.

The subsequent court of inquiry noted how different the outcome might have been if the aircraft had been available earlier. It would possibly have been able to pinpoint the exact whereabouts of the *Princess Victoria* to the lifeboats and commercial vessels in the area who were trying to help. The fact that its engines were running, if very slowly, meant that the ferry had moved away from the location from which the first calls were made, out towards Ireland, hindering the small armada of rescuers from finding it in the atrocious conditions. Early transmission had given the position of the disabled ship as 5 miles north-west of Corsewall Point, but those slowly turning engines – they eventually stopped at 1.08 p.m. – and the effect of the storms meant that when the order to abandon ship was given at around 2 p.m. she was 5 miles east of the Copeland Islands, three small islands to the north of Donaghadee. The officers on the bridge had believed they were still a good distance offshore until they glimpsed Ireland through the storm.

All disasters are said to be an unlucky combination of circumstances. The *Princess Victoria* was no exception. All sorts of bits of misfortune contributed to the loss of life. The Hasting aircraft was not in the right place at the right time, though that was no fault of the RAF. Even the first ship near the scene, HMS *Launceston Castle*, which was carrying out searches for survivors, had to leave the scene owing to mechanical problems. Another naval vessel, HMS *Tenacious*, based in Ireland and not many miles from the scene of the sinking, was singled out for criticism in the court of inquiry since it was not able to put to sea because too many crew members had been given shore leave. In the tradition of shutting the door after the horse had bolted, this led to a destroyer being stationed at Lough Foyle and kept on constant readiness to put to sea in an hour if a similar emergency was to occur.

Even when HMS *Contest* arrived at the scene the visibility was so bad that it could not see the ferry. *Contest* had made a daring high-speed dash to the rescue area from the Firth of Clyde holiday resort of Rothesay on the Isle of Bute, where it had been berthed. For a time it battled into huge seas at its top speed of 31 knots, but damage from the ferocious waves forced the destroyer's skipper, Lt Commander H.P. Fleming, to reduce speed to 16 knots.

The Portpatrick lifeboat *Jeannie Spiers* was also sent out into the storm. And the Donaghadee lifeboat *Sir Samuel Kelly* (later preserved and put into a collection at the Ulster Folk and Transport Museum) was also involved. The fierce storms that day had driven four small merchant ships to shelter in Belfast Lough and when they heard the transmission for help from a position not far from where they were they put to sea to give any assistance they could. These vessels were the cattle ship *Lairdsmoor*, the Fleetwood trawler *Eastcotes*, a smallish oil tanker, the *Pass of Drumochter*, and a coastal cargo ship, the *Orchy*.

These rescue ships were nearer the sinking area than either of the life boats or HMS *Contest*, and *Orchy* arrived on the disaster scene first. There was little the ships could do – they could not rescue any survivors in the lifeboats, as the huge waves were liable to dash the small boats against the side of the larger boats. They did, however, give some shelter in the heavy seas until the *Sir Samuel Kelly* arrived and managed to get some survivors aboard. The master of the *Orchy*, who was later awarded a medal for his bravery, gave his radio operator a message to relay: 'There are a lot of people here but they cannot get hold of the line. Position hopeless. Cannot lower lifeboats but doing our best. The ship will not do anything for us.'

The weather was still vile, with blinding squalls of sleet and rain hampering visibility and making the RAF's efforts to drop rubber dinghies difficult. A crew member of one of the lifeboats remembers spending two hours searching for survivors, and one man was found clinging to a raft on which were four other people who had died of exposure. The first survivors were taken to Donaghadee. One said: 'I didn't expect to be alive . . . I was in the lower deck when the boat started to go over and I scrambled down the side of it and got into a lifeboat. We pushed away with about twenty on board and managed to pick a few out of the sea. We did not have oars; the sea just took its course.'

There were no women and children among the forty-four survivors. There were reports of a lifeboat with women and children being overwhelmed by the waves and of another smashed to matchwood against the side of the ship. A grim scene. The cruel sea is no respecter of wealth, power or fame. Families of ordinary folk were drowned alongside high-ranking politicians and other dignitaries.

A court of inquiry was held into the sinking in March 1953 at Crumlin Road Courthouse in Belfast and produced a report of 30,000 pages that was a mixture of technical detail and stories of human bravery. On the technical side it declared that the stern doors were not up to the job (the blame for this lay with the builders) and in addition the arrangements for clearing water from the car deck were inadequate.

On the human side, the report remarked: 'If the *Princess Victoria* had been as staunch as those who manned her, then all would have been well and the disaster averted.' Looking back, this bravery is the most striking aspect of the story. After all, the *Princess Victoria's* was a pioneering design and in any field the newest of the new inevitably has problems: this applies to massive IT projects, supersonic aircraft and roll-on roll-off ferries alike. The errors that caused the disaster are not unique – two other ferries of the same type, the MS *Jan Heweliusz* and the MS *Estonia*, sank in 1993 and 1994 respectively, in storms that they should have survived, while the MS *Herald of Free Enterprise*, which capsized moments after leaving port in 1987, foundered largely because of human error.

Real bravery was shown by both rescuers and crew. In October 1953 the *London Gazette* announced the award of the British Empire Medal to Captain James Alexander Bell, Master of the *Lairdsmoor* (Portavogie, Co. Down), David Brewster, skipper of the fishing trawler *Eastcotes* (North Fleetwood), Captain James Kelly, Master of the *Pass of Drumochter* (Carnlough, Co. Antrim) and Captain Hugh Angus Mathieson, Master of the *Orchy* (Glasgow).

One of those who lost his life in the disaster was the radio officer of the *Princess Victoria*, David Broadfoot. The highest award for bravery that can be given to a civilian is the George Cross, and at Buckingham Palace Mrs Muriel

Broadfoot of Stranraer, accompanied by her thirteen-year-old son William, attended an investiture and received the George Cross awarded to her late husband. The citation was remarkable: 'From the moment when the *Princess Victoria* first got into difficulties, Radio Officer Broadfoot constantly sent out messages giving the ship's position and asking for assistance. The severe list the vessel had taken, and which was gradually increasing, rendered his task even more difficult. Despite the difficulties and danger, he steadfastly continued his work at the transmitting set, repeatedly sending signals to the coast radio station to enable them to ascertain the ship's exact position.'

There were also awards for the crew of the Portpatrick lifeboat, who also took huge risks in the rescue effort.

If there is one thing Scotland's rugged coast is not short of it is poignant memorials to loss of life at sea. Those who perished when the *Princess Victoria* went down are remembered in memorials at Larne, Portpatrick and Stranraer. The actual wreck lay undiscovered until 1992, when a team of divers from Cromarty Firth Diving located it in 90 metres of water near the Copeland Islands and video footage was shown in a BBC documentary.

An interesting footnote to the story of the *Princess Victoria* is the fact that in the years since there has never been a similar disaster, despite the thousands of journeys made each year by ferries plying the same route – often in vile weather – and the many other services that support life on the isles around our stormy coast. The safety of the ferries is further demonstrated by the fact that the only other major sinking was that of MacBrayne's *Loch Seaforth* in 1973. The *Loch Seaforth* was the biggest vessel in Calmac's fleet until the sixties, when ferries with superior car-loading facilities came on the scene, and was the only ship belonging to the line to be lost in passenger service. Maybe there had been signs that she was to have an untimely end – in her career she had been involved in groundings in Kyle, Mallaig and off Longay. The Mallaig incident had left her high and dry for two days. The final blow came in March 1973, when she hit Cleit Rock in the Sound of Gunna. Fortunately all the passengers got off safely and she was towed to Gott Bay, Tiree. But her difficult life had a final twist. When she was being pumped dry, a bulkhead collapsed and she sank, blocking the island's pier until May. Eventually she was raised and towed to Troon for scrapping. It is to be hoped that Calmac's new *Loch Seaforth*, launched in March 2014 in Germany and destined for the Ullapool–Stornoway route, currently serviced by the *Isle of Lewis*, has a less adventurous life.

As the *Princess Victoria* discovered, however, the Irish Sea can be a wild and unforgiving place, though the revolutionary design of the ship also played its part in the disaster. It is remarkable that anyone at all managed to survive this disaster in those appalling conditions. No doubt there were many on the football terraces where I was that day for whom this became a deep personal tragedy. There were others, too, who embarked the *Princess Victoria* that fateful day who could count themselves very lucky indeed.

2

THE DESTROYER THAT
TORPEDOED ITSELF

This book is a voyage back into the history of the toll that the cruel sea has taken on seafarers around Scotland's coast. Rather than tell the chosen tales in chronological order, it is a sort of geographical journey from the south-west (the Irish Sea) up through the Western Isles, round the almost always stormy Pentland Firth and down the east coast to the border. But like all journeys, the occasional diversion is called for.

I suppose the next nearest geographical point of disaster going north from the scene of the sinking of the *Princess Victoria* would be Sanda Island off the Mull of Kintyre, the graveyard of many a vessel, including its most famous victim, the American liberty ship the *Byron Darnton*. But that would involve crossing the mouth of the Firth of Clyde, that mighty indentation in the coastline, and forgetting the tragedies that have happened on these coastal waters, which are, in peaceful times, a paradise for yachtsmen and tourists.

The Clyde, perhaps the most famous and respected shipbuilding river in the world, streams through the heart of

Scotland's most populated and industrial city – Glasgow. It splits the city from north to south and for many years, before the construction of a wheen of bridges, the population on either side of the river depended on ferries. Down the years there were the famous vessels called Cluthas and also ungainly large vehicular ferries that plied the short distance to each bank.

But as far back as 1864 this crossing claimed lives. In November of that year one of the rowing-boat ferries then in use capsized and nineteen men were drowned. This very serious loss of life followed earlier losses from these small boats and resulted in the first powered ferries being intro-duced in 1865. At one time there were eleven landing stages and the Clutha plied up and down the river as well as across it, ferrying workers to and from shipyards and engineering works. They lost some of their usefulness when the city's subway system came into operation in 1896, passing under the Clyde from north to south, and they ceased to run in 1903. The name Clutha, incidentally, is said to come from the Latin for the name of the river.

The sheer volume of ferry traffic on the river was remark-able and it is not surprising that there were drownings. According to the Strathclyde Department of Education, the peak came around the beginning of the twentieth century, when, in addition to the Clutha, there were seven cross-river ferries in Glasgow harbour – at York Street, Clyde Street, Finnieston, Kelvinhaugh, Govan, Govan West and Whiteinch. A rowing-boat ferry also crossed the mouth of the Kelvin, another crossed the mouth of Queen's Dock on Sundays and a private ferry ran by permission of the city corporation from Oatlands to Glasgow Green. Some of the ferries ran twenty-four hours of the day. They were certainly exciting and dangerous times. There were even tales of ladies in crinolines crossing the river, standing on the seats to save crushing a valuable dress. Vanity never goes out of fashion!

Just a few miles down-river from the city centre, an early tragedy showed that the maritime environment could kill not only sailors and passengers, but also the men and boys who built the ships. The story of the launch of the *Daphne* in 1883 is now largely forgotten, but it involved great loss of life almost seconds after the ship first floated on the murky waters of the Clyde at Govan. It is also noteworthy that the disaster was witnessed by large crowds, many of whom lost relatives when the ship capsized. Nearly 200 workmen were on board the ship, a small coasting vessel, at the time of the launch, and of these 124 lost their lives.

Naturally a full inquiry followed and, as so often is the case in such happenings, a sensible recommendation resulted, though it was something that perhaps should have been realised earlier: that it would be prudent during a launch to have the minimum number of workers on board. The men on the *Daphne*, as it slid down the ways, were on station to get on with the fitting out immediately after the ship was in the water. Many need not have been there and their deaths were entirely unnecessary.

There are many accounts of this shipyard accident in the archives and one of the fullest versions can be found at Clydesite.co.uk. This source says:

As was usual in the launching of ships two anchors and cables were employed to check the way on the ship after she had entered the water. On this occasion the checking apparatus failed to function. The starboard anchor moved some six or seven yards but the port anchor dragged for about sixty yards and the

current of the river catching the ship at a critical moment
turned her over on her port side.

Most of the workers on board were trapped below deck, where they were ready to work even as the ship was towed to the fitting-out dock. Naturally, with so many folk in the area, a huge rescue effort was launched, but only around seventy survivors managed to get ashore. The speed of the capsize was partly due to many of the men on board sliding to the port side and the fact that 30 tons of loose gear were doing the same. Additionally, water entered the ship through a boiler-room hatch.

The *Daphne* sank in water so deep that it completely covered her at high tide. The inquiry, though wise after the event on the practice of having so many workers on board, did not seem to get to the root of the cause of such a disaster and it exonerated the builders, Alexander Stephen and Sons, of any blame – hard to believe since clearly the check equipment was at fault. This caused a huge controversy locally and the general opinion seemed to be that it was a 'whitewash'. Indeed, the builders were commended for the assistance they gave the inquiry. No fault was found with the launch arrangements at the Linthouse yard and the cause was said to be 'little initial stability combined with excessive loose gear and personnel aboard'. No fault of the builders? That has to be very much in question.

Most maritime tragedies take place in howling gales, high seas, rain, snow, sleet or crashing surf. But just down-river from where the *Daphne* capsized on launch more than 100 years ago, another incident claimed the lives of three members of a tugboat crew, the *Flying Phantom*, in waters almost as calm as the proverbial millpond.

Today, thousands of tourists and folk interested in the history of the Clyde travel to a refurbished area of riverbank in front of Clydebank College. In the main they are bound for a visit to the mighty Titan crane, which stands as a proud reminder of the great days of shipbuilding on the legendary river. One hundred and fifty feet high, it was used for lifting heavy items like engines and boilers in the fitting-out of battleships and giant liners at John Brown's yard. It was the largest crane of its type in the world when it was built and was used in the construction of the Queens, including the *Queen Elizabeth* and the *QE2*.

Now a 'category A' listed historical structure, it was refurbished in 2007 as a tourist attraction and shipbuilding museum and it makes a good destination for a visit. I made the journey there, myself on a fine July day and gazed across the Clyde from the area near the base of the crane. It was a pleasant spot in the sunshine, if a little noisy as the jets did their finals on the approach to Glasgow airport, and it was difficult to imagine the scene on the night of 19 December 2007.

The tug went down almost right opposite the college and crane. Despite the calm water the climate played a major role. This time it was freezing fog. The *Flying Phantom* was based in Greenock, where for generations folk sailing 'doon the watter' on holiday from Glasgow have admired the sturdy fleet of vessels waiting to ply their trade on the river. The *Flying Phantom* was similar in design to many others operating out of Greenock and looked to the layman tough, powerful and indestructible.

On the night of the tragedy the *Flying Phantom* was towing the 77,000-ton freighter *Red Jasmine* to help it dock. Visibility was appalling on the river, low temperature and that freezing fog making it difficult for both the freighter and the tug to see what was happening. The last radio contact with the tug was made just before 6 p.m., when the crew told the *Red Jasmine* pilot: 'We're stuck on the bank.' The pilot replied: 'Let go of the line then, please,' to which the *Flying Phantom* responded: 'Will do.' But as subsequent inquiries found out, a towing winch did not release quickly enough and the larger vessel pulled the tug under. It happened very quickly and only Brian Aitchison, thirty-seven, from Coldingham managed to escape from the tug's wheelhouse. The bodies of three other crew members – skipper Stephan Humphreys, thirty-three, of Greenock; Eric Blackley, fifty-seven, from Gourock; and Robert Cameron, sixty-five, from Houston – were later recovered. Tugmen call what happened to the *Flying Phantom* 'girting', meaning that it was pulled over by the ship it was towing.

One of the major differences in the aftermath of the two disasters, the *Daphne* and the *Flying Phantom*, which had happened so close to one another on a stretch of river not considered particularly dangerous, was the apportioning of blame. The tug's owner, Svitzer Marine, was fined £1.7m after pleading guilty to health-and-safety failures and admitting it failed to put in place a safe operating procedure after a grounding seven years previously. The judge, Lord Turnbull, told the High Court in Edinburgh that the fine would have been higher if the company had not pleaded guilty. He said: 'In identifying the particular level of fine I consider appropriate to the present case, I am not seeking to identify the level of worth of the individuals who lost their lives. Nor am I seeking to reflect in financial terms the meas-ure of loss suffered by their families.' In a sympathetic com-ment he continued: 'In the end of the day any sentence imposed by me will likely seem insignificant compared to the sentence they have had imposed on them.' He told the court that victims' families 'will have to face an entirely different future from the ones they had looked forward to spending with husbands, fathers and grandfathers'.

Svitzer admitted 'failing to ensure, as far as reasonably practicable, the health, safety and welfare at work' of the crew, an important admission when decent sensible treatment of a workforce can be criticised and dismissed by pundits of the health-and-safety culture. In this case, had the company not failed on this issue, lives could have been saved. Pat Rafferty of Unite, the deceased men's union, was critical of the time taken to come to a conclusion as to what had happened and the fact that the judge could not 'legally enforce changes to working practices that could prevent future fatalities'.

The various investigations also highlighted the surprising fact that there were no defined procedures when assisting or towing in restricted visibility. There was also at the time no industry standard for tug towline emergency-release systems. And the mechanical failure of a winch was the prime cause of the disaster. The Clydeport authorities were also criticised for not having a designated person in charge of safety measures and for the fact that few control measures had been put in place after a previous similar serious accident in thick fog. Many official actions are criticised for only improving land, sea and air safety conditions after there have been fatal accidents. But learning a lesson on safety from an incident is always worthwhile. It is interesting that recently there have been calls for another inquiry into this accident.

If wind and storm had little to do with the tug tragedy, a few further miles down-river there is physical evidence of what a tempest can do. Indeed, the wreck of what is called the 'sugar' boat is there for all to see. And you don't even have to go out in a dinghy or cabin cruiser to see what is one of the sights of the Clyde. You can even catch a glimpse of the upturned hull of the MV *Captayannis* from the comfort of the Helensburgh to Glasgow train. And in certain tidal conditions it can be seen from towns on both sides of the river.

There was, luckily, no loss of life, but the sinking of the freighter was potentially more dangerous than the mere loss of an elderly vessel. The ship had been built in Greece in 1946 as the *Norden* but was renamed in 1963. When it sank in 1974, the sugar-refining industry in Greenock was winding down. In the late 1880s and '90s it is said that the astonishing figure of around 400 ships a year delivered unrefined sugar from the Caribbean plantations to the Scottish refineries. At one time the town had around a dozen sugar factories, but the Caribbean connection – which stretched back to 1765 – ended in 1997 when the sole survivor, Tate & Lyle, closed their factory.

The *Captayannis* had arrived at the Tail of the Bank, often a busy anchorage, on the evening of 27 January 1974. She dropped anchor and waited to deliver her sweet cargo to the James Watt dock. But a ferocious storm blew up, the Greek ship's chain began to drag and she ended up colliding with another vessel, the BP tanker *British Light*. The tanker was robust enough to sustain no serious damage from the drifting ship, but her anchor chain fatally holed the sugar boat and water began to pour in. The captain of the *Captayannis* acted swiftly and tried to make for the sheltered waters of the Gareloch on the north side of the Firth. Before he could get near this place of safety he realised that the water was coming in so fast that his ship was in imminent danger of sinking under him. Again thinking fast, he took a decision that probably saved the lives of those on board – he beached his ship on a sandbank in shallow waters near the north shore.

Out into the wild night sailed a small flotilla of rescuers, pilot boats, the tug *Labrador* and Clyde Marine's small passenger vessel the *Rover*. The sugar boat was stuck fast on the sand and keeled over at such an angle that it was possible for twenty-five members of the crew to simply jump from the *Captayannis* onto the *Rover* and safety. They were taken ashore, but the skipper and four other members of the crew boarded the tug.

The next morning the vessel rolled over on her side and that was that. She was not in a position to be a threat to navigation, but in normal circumstances she would have been towed off the sandbank and broken up. This did not happen because of a long-running dispute over who owned her and who would have to pay salvage costs. And a plan to blow her up was dropped because of the danger to a nearby bird sanctuary at Ardmore Point. So, there she lies to this day. Over the years what you might call looters have stripped the hulk of anything they thought might earn a bob or two, or make a good souvenir. The only value of the wreck now is as a home to marine bird life.

If the upturned hull of the sugar boat is an iconic part of the seascape of the north side of the Firth, then across from it is an equally striking reminder of the past – the memorial to the Free French forces high on the Lyle Hill above Greenock. At around 500 feet above sea level the memorial can be seen from miles around, an attractive piece of sculpture combining the Cross of Lorraine and an anchor. Ask most folk about it – even in Greenock, Gourock and Port Glasgow – and many will tell you that it is a memorial to the French sailors who died in an accidental explosion on the destroyer *Maillé Brézé*, which was anchored off the Tail of the Bank in April 1940. It is a nice tale but not correct. When the *Maillé Brézé* blew up, the Free French force had not officially come into being – though it did so some months later – and there is no mention of the sailors on the monument, which is dedicated to the larger part played in the war by the Free French in Scotland.

There is a much less imposing, though more specific, memorial to the men of the *Maillé Brézé*, who died in one of the most horrific incidents in the war, at Brookwood military cemetery in Surrey, England. The actual figures of the death toll vary in the archives. Some sources have it that six died on the upper deck and thirty below deck and that forty-seven were hospitalised. Others offer slightly lower figures.

No one can really be sure of the total number of casualties, but the story of the explosion itself is extraordinary. The 2,400-ton destroyer was sunk by one of her own torpedoes while at anchor. This sort of accident is not quite so unusual as it sounds, as in wartime accidental explosions are always a danger. In the First World War a shipping accident in Nova Scotia created the largest man-made explosion before the invention of nuclear weapons. In 1917 a French cargo vessel, the *Monte-Blanc*, fully loaded with explosives, collided with a Norwegian ship, *Imo*, in a narrow strait connecting Halifax Harbour and Bedford Basin. A fire started on the ammunition carrier and twenty minutes after the collison the ammunition blew up. Around 2,000 were killed and almost 10,000 injured in the blast, which started fires, collapsed buildings onshore and hurled debris over a vast area.

Such accidents were not confined to ships. Although not on the scale of the Halifax incident, aviation buffs remember one legendary American test pilot who can claim to be perhaps the only man to have shot himself out of the air. Testing a missile on a fighter jet, it malfunctioned and brought his plane down. He survived.

Not so lucky were many of the crew of the destroyer *Maillé Brézé*. The warship had returned to Greenock for maintenance after duties escorting the battleship *Bretagne* and the cruiser *Algerie,* who had been tasked with taking the French nation's gold reserves to Canada for safekeeping. Back in the Clyde she was anchored in the crowded waters of the Tail of the Bank, taking on ammunition.

The *Maillé Brézé* was at the top end of the destroyer class, almost large enough to be classified as a light cruiser. This formidable fighting vessel had a remarkable top speed of 37 knots, but the accident happened when she was stationary. She carried torpedoes on deck as part of her armament and on a pleasant spring afternoon in April 1940 the unthinkable happened. The torpedoes were not in line but 'staggered' on the deck, trained fore and aft when at rest. Without warning one armed weapon was launched, owing, it was thought, to a malfunction in the firing apparatus, and it leapt across the deck, setting fire to fuel tanks and the forward magazine, which fortunately did not explode immediately.

Like the death toll, the reasons given for the accident vary. The most accepted account has it that a torpedo tube had been turned inwards for maintenance and a live weapon accidentally fired inward and downwards into the hull. Other accounts say a live torpedo was dropped as it was being moved and exploded when it hit the deck. Whatever the reason, the explosion echoed around the Firth of Clyde and up into the Renfrewshire hills. One prominent Greenockian, now an internationally famous surgeon, was a schoolboy on the day of the disaster and he told me he remembers the afternoon well. Without a care in the world, he was heading for a sweet shop high in the housing area above the harbour when he heard the frightening sound of high explosives going off and the sight of smoke and flames rising into the air. Like everyone in the riverbank towns of Greenock, Port Glasgow and Gourock, he knew something appalling had happened.

When the safety mechanism failed, the torpedo slithered across the deck, colliding with the bridge structure. The fuel oil and anything else combustible was burning, even the forward magazine, and most of the forward part of the ship was torn to bits. A handful of sailors were killed by the immediate explosion and perhaps they were the lucky ones. Many of the crew were below decks at the time and as the ship burned the intense heat warped entrances and exits to the mess decks. Behind the twisted steel and flames sailors died a horrible death, and there were stories of would-be rescuers hearing the screams of the trapped as they clawed at portholes in vain attempts to escape. It was a navy man's worst nightmare.

All the small boats in Albert Harbour, close to the navy's headquarters in the area, were sent out to assist. The aircraft carrier HMS *Furious* was anchored close to the stricken French warship and a rescue party led by Lt D.S. Johnston was sent across to the destroyer. This group included a doctor and a sickbay attendant. The party climbed up the *Maillé Brézé*'s anchor chain to get aboard. Amid intense heat and smoke they realised that the men below were trapped with no hope of escape and were slowly burning to death. The doctor is reported to have given huge doses of morphine to any sailors who could get their arms out of the portholes. Eventually the deck became too hot to stay and the party had to retreat, with the doctor passing syringes and morphine through the portholes to the men dying in agony.

Another naval vessel, HMS *Barfield*, moored nearby started its engines and headed for the *Maillé Brézé*, steaming into an area that was like a chaotic firestorm, with shells shooting into the air and exploding. The whole area was a confusion of rescuers and large warships and tankers trying to move out of the danger presented by the burning destroyer still with so much ammunition on board. The *Barfield*, a smallish boom defence vessel, bravely tried to get alongside and use its fire hoses, but a large explosion from the French vessel drove it off.

The archives tell the story of another vessel involved in the rescue, HMS *Firedrake*. Since the incident started at lunchtime most of the crew of this vessel were in the wardroom eating when they heard the colossal explosion. But almost immediately they had two whalers in the water heading for the scene. The first lieutenant took one and a sub lieutenant another, with a doctor and coxswain. One whaler went to the bow to help men on the deck and fifteen men slid down the hawse pipe and were saved. The whaler with the doctor on board went along amidships and the coxswain, Peter Armstrong, hurled a medical chest from the boat up onto the deck, a feat of strength and dexterity. In the aftermath of the tragedy he was awarded the BEM. The *Firedrake* men who got on board found dead and dying

27

everywhere and amid this hellish scene they gave what medical help they could.

The first explosion happened at 2.15 p.m., but by 4 p.m. the ready-to-use ammunition had all exploded. There was by now no one left on board alive. Another rescue vessel, the tug *Marauder*, tried to take the wreck in tow, as it was still afloat despite the damage, though low in the water and sinking fast. The bow was still red hot and the forward magazine had not exploded. It was five and a half hours after the incident started that the destroyer finally sank by the bow to lie clear of the main navigation channel. Before the sinking a few sailors had returned on board to flood the aft magazine and the fire was eventually controlled by firemen from Greenock.

The bravery of all involved in the rescue was of the highest level. The rescuers sailed without thought of their own safety to aid stricken seafarers. The main magazines could have exploded at any moment and the loss of life would been massive. It was only in 1954 that the wreck of the *Maillé Brézé* was raised and the remains of the crew in the forecastle removed with full naval honours, after which a mass was held in St Lawrence's Church in the east end of Greenock. The remains of the sailors were taken to France and at last the warriors who suffered such a dreadful death could rest in peace in their native land. Their ship was taken to breakers in Port Glasgow.

A rather sad tailpiece is the fact that reports written in the aftermath of the disaster noted that, 'Since that day escape hatches have been fitted in mess decks of all small ships.' Not for the first time in this narrative of the toll of Scotland's cruel sea, the remedial action came too late for many.

3

K13: WHAT WERE
THEY THINKING ABOUT?

Tragic accidents in the Firth of Clyde are far from confined to the upper river or around the Tail of the Bank. The waters westward towards the open Atlantic, after the great shipyards of Port Glasgow and Greenock fall away on the port side, have taken a toll down the years, mostly as a result of submarine incidents or accidents related to great storms – though weather is not always a factor. Though there are plenty of shipwrecks in the open Atlantic, which I will come to later in this book, there were many more in the upper river in addition to the *Daphne* and *Maillé Brézé* disasters.

The grounding of the world's last seagoing paddle steamer, the *Waverley*, on the Gantocks, a group of small rocks just south of the holiday resort of Dunoon, may not have cost lives or have been as traumatic as many another sea disaster, but it was a significant reminder that when at sea, even on a calm July day in Scotland, potential disaster is never far away. The *Waverley*, still going strong in 2014, was almost fatally damaged on that summer's day in 1977.

No one was hurt, but the iconic vessel was badly damaged and for a time it was thought its career was over.

Down the years the Gantocks, despite having a beacon on them, have snagged many a small ship, mostly without loss of life though three crewmen died when a freighter hit them in the forties. The *Waverley* incident in 1977 came at a time when its peculiarities with regard to its steering had begun to cause some concern to the crew. But it still seemed inexplicable that such a thing should happen.

Almost within sight of the Gantocks in the upper Firth, a remarkable and, in this case, tragic submarine accident occurred in the Gareloch in January 1917. Of all the tales told in this book, the story of *K13* is without any doubt the most bizarre. Looking back, it is clear that the blame lay with the Admiralty top brass who threw common sense out of the Whitehall windows and pursued a mad scheme that was never for a moment going to work safely.

It defies belief that the K-class of submarines was ever built. When the First World War broke out – and in the months before the start of hostilities – the Royal Navy was obsessed with a race against Germany to build bigger and better battleships. The fact that the potential enemy had been building up a huge fleet of submarines was ignored until the out-of-touch former public schoolboys who ran the show belatedly realised that our merchant fleet was taking a bit of a pounding from German subs. Not only that, the enemy had plans for huge ocean-going subs capable of 22 knots on the surface. The so-called elite then made their one correct decision on subs at that time. They determined we had to build a class of large, high-speed ocean-going submarines of our own. This was to be the K-class. The decision to build such subs may have been the right one in principle, but the design was a disatrous error.

Incidentally, these subs were not dignified by name, rather merely numbered, something I suspect was because the Admiralty top brass had a hang-up on the use of submarines, preferring to glory in battleships. Submarines were thought just the dastardly sort of weapon that only the Hun would use. Creeping up unseen under the water and sinking civilian ships and drowning non-combatants by the hundred was just not cricket. There was another example of such thinking during the Second World War when Churchill, now no longer First Lord of the Admiralty but prime minister, realised that the Germans would use every dirty trick in the book against us and called on General Lucky Laycock to form the Commandos, a group as skilled in the dark arts of war as the enemy. If the Germans would not play by the rules, neither should we. A good decision, indeed.

However, in the First World War the way the decision-makers went about coming to terms with submarine warfare could have come straight out of a Monty Python sketch when they decreed that the subs would be steam-powered. One prominent American naval historian, Edward C. Whitman, said of this decision:

The Royal Navy's K-class submarines were perhaps the most badly conceived and ill-starred submersibles ever built by any nation. In both their original configuration and in several derivatives that followed, the K-boats compiled an almost unbroken record of disaster and death, unredeemed by even a single incidence of combat effectiveness. Spawned by a flawed tactical concept, implemented with immature and dangerous

31

technologies, and kept at sea by the Admiralty's stubborn refusal to admit the most obvious deficiencies, the K-class left in their wake a fascinating – even humorous – tale of operational and technical folly for which the query, 'what were they thinking?' has seldom been more appropriate.

A five-year-old could have worked out that steam boilers and submarines with funnels that folded before they dived was never going to be a good idea.

Until that moment of folly, British subs had been diesel-powered and we did not have one faster than 16 knots. But, to be fair to the navy brass, it should be pointed out that some at the top did express concerns about the basic concept of using steam power. But the subs were built anyway.

The statistics of *K13* are impressive: almost 2,000 tons surfaced (2,566 submerged), it was 339 feet long with a beam of 26.5 feet and a draft of an inch under 21 feet. So far so good, but the propulsion were Twin 10,500-shp oil-fired Yarrow boilers each powering a Brown-Curtis or Parson geared steam turbine. When dived there were four powerful electric motors. There was also an 800 hp diesel generator for charging the batteries when surfaced. This particular vessel was ordered from Fairfield in Govan, Glasgow, in August 1915 and launched on 11 November 1916. Then the problems began.

That there was trouble ahead should have been no surprise. All those of a superstitious nature would have given note to the number *K13*, but there was more solid cause for concern in the incidents involving previously launched vessels of the same class. Explosions, fuel leaks, boiler flashbacks and groundings were common. Examples are the refusal of *K6* to surface during a static dive at Devonport

Dockyard and a later incident involving *K14* when the batteries were flooded and the crew were lucky to escape being gassed to death. This particular happening was hushed up in wartime. Indeed, if the whole record of the K-class had been public knowledge I wonder how many would have voluntarily served on them!

But war was war and the *K13* began sea trials in the Gareloch. She was designed to have a crew of six officers and fifty-three ratings. But there were eighty on board on the day of the disaster, 29 January 1917: fifty-three navy crew, fourteen Fairfield employees, five sub-contractors, five Admiralty officials, a River Clyde pilot, and the captain and engineering officer of *K14*, which was still being worked on by the builders. I suspect there must have been some anxiety for those on board, for some of them at least would have known the K-class's record of accidents before its fatal dive. It would have been hard around Clydeside to completely hide the story of a previous trial, when heavy seas damaged one of the funnels and the engine room was nearly flooded by water rushing into the vessel. In fact, the real trouble with the K-class boats was what veteran submariners called 'too many holes'.

Filmgoers will be conscious in the transition from surface travel to underwater travel of the obvious need to make the boat watertight before diving – almost every submarine drama ever made has a soundtrack of frantic klaxons blaring and shouts of 'Dive! Dive!', plus shots of watertight doors being frantically screwed shut as the last drops of salty seawater trickle down the conning tower and into the command post as the skipper checks with all and sundry that the ship is safe to dive. It was a matter of life and death. But on a K-class it was not a relatively simple matter of screwing a couple hatches shut. Those ludicrous funnels had to be stowed and there were many other 'holes', mainly ventilators – necessitated by the mad folly of using steam power – to be closed and checked.

Incidentally, there was another flaw in a design: using oil-fired boilers. They created too much heat in the vessel, heat that was almost unbearable in the engine room, and because of the positioning of the boilers, communication between stern and bow sections was most difficult. Reports at the time called the K-class 'super' subs and for a time *K13* was the fastest submarine in the world, with a surface speed of 23 knots. But at a great price. Conditions for the crew, even on the surface, were horrific, the process of diving took an age and all the ventilators and paraphernalia made human error almost inevitable. A more appropriate adjective to 'super' would be 'killer'.

The day of the tragedy started gently. At around 8 a.m. in Fairfield's yard the order to cast off was given by the skipper, Commander Godfrey Herbert, and the huge sub was pulled out of its berth by tugs into the calm waters of the River Clyde, a few miles from the city centre. Under its own power it headed west for the test area at the Gareloch. Surface trials, and an early dive, went well, and in the great tradition of the navy and its upper-class officers, the next important event before more diving tests was lunch. This was said to have been enjoyed in 'festive mood', despite the fact that those in the know realised how flawed their sub was.

It was 3.15 p.m. before the sub was steered to the dive area. Then the routine of testing that the instrumentation was working took place. With the exception of one flickering instrument, all seemed well. The flickering was put down to a wiring problem, but in fact it showed that there was a problem with the boiler-room ventilators. Reports after the accident say that four were left open to the sea as *K13* submerged. At first the sub dived smoothly, but it was supposed to level out at a depth of six metres. This did not happen and it continued to head down into the deep. Frantic efforts were made to stop this plunge. The hydroplanes were moved to 'hard a rise' in an effort to get back to the surface and the sub was filled with the noise of screaming compressed air as the ballast tanks were cleared of water. Even the forward keel, weighing ten tons, was dropped. But within seconds the officers were told that the boiler room was flooding fast, no doubt with water pouring into the hull through the faulty ventilators. The fact that this was happening as a result of the stupidity of a design that required air that was carried into the boiler room when the sub was on the surface was by now academic. A hard decision had to be made. The watertight doors between the boiler room and the rest of the vessel had to be closed immediately. This meant certain death for those trapped behind it, but it had to be done to prevent an even greater loss of life. The commanding officer ordered the doors closed and it was done. Thirty-one lives were lost by this action.

But the disaster continued to build. The sub careered on down into the depths, where it settled stern down in 15 metres of water. As if that wasn't enough to contend with, a sudden fire broke out on a switchboard and only frantic efforts by the crewmen put it out, but not before it had consumed some of the oxygen needed for the trapped men to survive until rescuers arrived. And that, as we will see, took a long time.

Gradually, as the sub failed to appear, observers realised something was wrong. A further sign was the oil slicks appearing on the surface. It took until 10 p.m. for the first rescue vessel, the *Gossamer*, to arrive at the scene. This was despite the fact that an escorting tug had radioed an urgent message suggesting a disaster was imminent. If there was panic and fear down below, the scene on the surface, if the sub's crew could have seen it, was not a helpful one. It took six hours, during which valuable oxygen was being consumed, before a gunboat and salvage tugs were dispatched to the scene.

Clearly a search by divers was needed, but no suitable diving suit was on board the *Gossamer* and when one was found it was so perished it almost drowned the would-be rescuer who put it on. Finally a civilian diver from the builders Fairfield got to the trapped vessel and communicated with the survivors by hammering out messages in Morse code on the hull. *K13* was embedded in the muddy bottom; presumably it had been going hard when driven into the sand. It turned out that the early attempts to stop the dive by dropping the ballast keel had failed. The sub had been out of control and heading down fast when it had hit the bottom.

As mentioned, *K13* had two commanders on board: the sub's own skipper Captain Godfrey Herbert and Captain Goodhart of *K14*. Heads were put together as the trapped men waited for help and all sorts of plans discussed. Eventually the two captains decided on a dicey plan that would put one man on the surface, if successful, and help the rescuers. The idea was for Goodhart to escape through the conning tower and be propelled upwards by a bubble of compressed air. Herbert was to supervise the operation. However, the burst of compressed air took both by surprise and Goodhart was forced at high speed into the steel of the conning tower and was killed instantly. Herbert was then himself swept up to the surface in the powerful rush of the compressed air and was picked up by the salvage crew. He and his crew were lucky in this. Herbert's knowledge of the innards of the sub was to be of valuable help in saving the survivors. Experts were now working out how long any air left in *K13* would stay breathable before the crew suffocated. 'Not long' was the answer and it was a race against time.

The divers went down and again managed to communicate with those below the waves by means of tapping on the hull using Morse code. This time they managed to connect a small hose through which some air, food and drink was passed. In a rather surprising human touch, playing cards were also transferred into the sub to help pass the time for the men who must have been waiting in an agony of suspense and fear.

The salvage was tricky. A plan was formed to feed wire hawsers round the nose of the sub and winch the bow up above the level of the water. Captain Herbert thought at this point that the survivors could then escape through the torpedo tubes. However, even a relatively simple plan like this presented immense difficulties. The first phase of the plan did finally work, and the bow was slowly raised towards the surface. But just as it finally looked like a success, the sub suddenly slipped back down just below the surface of the water. Clearly, escape through the torpedo tube was now impossible.

The only option then left was to cut through the hull, a precarious and time-consuming operation in any conditions. But, finally, they cut through and the men who remained alive managed a remarkable escape from what had looked to be an impossible situation. The forty-eight survivors had been trapped for fifty-seven hours when they crawled out to gulp in fresh air and appreciate their luck.

The death toll was thirty-two, including six civilians from Fairfield. When the time came to remove the bodies from the flooded aftersection, there was a surprise since it was thought that there would be thirty-one corpses (Captain Goodhart's body was trapped in the conning tower) but in fact there were only twenty-nine. The solution to this puzzle is ironic. In the period when *K13* went missing, a maid in a local hotel reported seeing two men in the water but was ignored by the authorities. Had she been taken seriously it could have been helpful in the rescue attempt. The men in the water turned out to have been two crewmen who had managed to get out of the aft section as the sub sank. Some months later, one of the bodies was found.

The death of the brave men who took to sea in such an unsuitable vessel is commemorated in at least three impressive memorials. The one most familiar to Glaswegians is in Elder Park, Govan, a stone's throw from where *K13* was built. This was not erected until some years after the accident. Fairfield workers had contributed to the cost and in a ceremony Sir Alexander Kennedy paid tribute to those who had died in what was still being described as a 'super submarine'. And some further details of what took place on the day of the tragedy were revealed. *The Herald* put it this way: 'Owing to an overlook on the part of someone who paid for his mistake with his life, four large ventilators leading to the boiler room were left open.' The report also paid tribute to the work of Captain Herbert in the rescue operation. And Sir Alexander had some words of special appreciation for the civilians who died. He said: 'They lost their lives when engaged in the final testing of a naval weapon which had been constructed for the purpose of overcoming our enemies and securing national safety.' In a reference to the troubled times post the First World War, he added, 'Something of the same spirit and courage as these men showed were required today in support of the active cooperation of men of good-will who were trying to win through the trade depression which was causing much anxiety in the community.'

There is also a memorial to the men of *K13* at the entrance to Faslane cemetery. And in faraway New South Wales there is another memorial at Carlingford. This was paid for by the widow of Charles Freestone, a leading telegraphist on *K13* who survived and later went to a new life in Australia. This was unveiled in September 1961 – an impressive piece of work, it has a water feature and a sort of cairn, higher than a man, with the dedication '*K13*'. The inscription reads: 'This memorial has been created in memory of those officers and men of the Commonwealth who gave their lives in submar-ines while serving the cause of freedom.' Such memorials are of immense value in preserving the memory of what happened during the Great War, particularly events that were hushed up at the time or perhaps overshadowed by the slaughter in the trenches.

And *K13*? It was refitted and repaired and renamed *K22*. It features in another remarkable story, known as the Battle of May Island, to be recounted later in this book when our voyage round Scotland's cruel sea reaches the Fife coast. But it would be wrong to end this chapter without a final word on steam-powered submersibles. Now they roam the oceans and are perhaps the most lethal weapons known to man. But no burning oil is in use, they have no funnels and no clouds of oily black smoke trail in their wake . . . Today's steam-powered giants belonging to the world's most advanced navies use nuclear reactors to generate the steam.

It is, of course, hardly necessary to point out that a career in submarines and the possibility of a slow, agonising death under the waves is something that most people, even those who consider themselves completely unafraid of enclosed spaces, find unattractive. But there has been, from the early days of steam-powered and diesel subs right up to the menacing nuclear monsters of today, a special breed of sailor who prefers the unpredictable adventure of plunging deep down in the oceans to the less dangerous life on the waves above in vessels where you can see the horizon, the clouds and the sky, and sniff the salt in the air. In almost all nations the men who man the submarines are volunteers. These men have a curious pride in their profession and are somewhat less than impressed by their fellows serving in conventional warships. The submariners dismiss their fellow navy men as 'skimmers'.

'Camaraderie' is a greatly overused word when describing military matters. But it exists anywhere a group of men are thrown together to fight as a unit. And nowhere is it more demonstrably a fact of life than in submarine crews. Each man is dependent on the skill and nerve of his fellows, from the commanding officer down to the ordinary seaman. And they operate in a testing environment. The old subs were crowded, smelly places often prone to leaks and constant dampness, but they at least could surface when safe to do so, to recharge the batteries and suck a little fresh air into the boat. And good skippers liked to let a seaman or two climb a slippery seaweed-encrusted ladder inside the 'sail' up onto the conning tower for a breath or two of fresh air. Today's nuclear boomers can be at sea for months on end without surfacing or refuelling or the crew breathing truly natural fresh air. It is a strange underwater world with no night and no day. The crews of the 'skimmers' get letters from home, watch TV news and live a life that is almost constantly in touch with the ordinary world. Not so on a nuclear sub. Incidentally, the nuclear subs in both the US and British navies have their own nickname – 'boomers' – which comes from the B and M in their full title: Fleet Ballistic Missile Submarines. I had a brief taste of life on the 'boomer' HMS *Vanguard* courtesy of the Ministry of Defence.

The top men in the modern Royal Navy are well aware of the problems of the strange, secretive life submariners are called to lead. When out on months-long patrols, even the news of the death of a loved one has to wait until the return to harbour. There may be a tiny mess and the occasional small beer in it for off-duty men, but it is not exactly the night at the pub that 'skimmers' can enjoy. The food may be excellent these days and even the air that fills the 'tin can' of the undersea boat tastes fresh, thanks to modern technology, but it is a strange, unreal world. Good mental health, as TV's favourite shrink Dr Frasier Crane might say, is a must for those who travel under the world's oceans with a cargo of nuclear weapons that could destroy millions of lives. But it is only natural for any man in the sub, living in crowded areas squeezed between nuclear weapons forward and the nuclear reactor aft, to worry and wonder what his family and friends are up to onshore during his long absences. Likewise, those family and friends wonder what life is like for their loved ones far away patrolling the seas on a mission to maintain world peace. So, from time to time, the Admiralty arranges short trips on the subs for some family and friends, so that they can better imagine life on the boat and maybe sweep away some misconceptions. For a wife or partner far distant from their man, an insight into his day-to-day life on the sub can assuage loneliness.

So it was that a few years ago I boarded *Vanguard* off Gourock, under the watchful eye of a sailor in camouflage bearing what looked to the layman like a tommy gun or its modern successor, and made course south down the Firth of Clyde for underwater hours in the deep area known as the Arran Trench and some cruising around Inchmarnock Island. It was an eye-opener both to life on a modern sub and to what it must have been like on an evil-smelling diesel sub, never mind an oil-fired K-class vessel. I admired the camaraderie – that word again – and the bravery of the crews. When my brief stay was over, I climbed the metal ladder out through a hatch onto the open deck, covered with anechoic tiles to improve secrecy undersea of the huge machine of mass destruction and breathed fresh air and enjoyed the view as a specially designed sub tender took us back to the comfortable safety of Helensburgh Pier and the delights of that lovely Clydeside town.

There's no doubt that it is a special kind of person who takes on the rigours of life as a submariner and this is true of both the early days of the K-class vessels and, for the months on end spent at sea in the nuclear-powered behemoths we have today.

4

THE MYSTERY OF THE SUBMARINE
THAT VANISHED

The Firth of Clyde is a huge tourist attraction. On sunlit summer days flotillas of yachts large and small – and more frequently now giant liners, most of which tend to look like floating skyscrapers rather than real ships – cruise the sparkling waters in the shadow of the mountains of Arran and Kintyre. This is one of the best sailing areas in the world, but you do not need to own an expensive yacht or 'gin palace' to enjoy it – the legendary west coast firm Caledonian MacBrayne and their rivals up the Firth, Western Ferries, give lots of opportunities to explore this holiday paradise from the deck of a ferry. One of the CalMac routes from Lochranza on the north-west of Arran to Clonaig on the Kintyre Peninsula is particularly spectacular.

To scenery as beautiful as any in the world is added the attraction of wildlife watching. The whales in the Kilbrannan Sound are infrequent and do not rival the humpbacks of Cape Cod, but they can be seen on occasion, as can dolphins more regularly and a fine assortment of seabirds. But the major attraction is basking sharks. The area off the

Lochranza–Clonaig route is a world heritage site for these awesome creatures. A few miles down the east side of the Kintyre Peninsula, at Carradale, the remnants of a shark-fishing industry can still be found, a few rusting boilers for extracting the once valuable oil. And in the pubs you might still hear tales of the shark fishing, including the astonishing account of the small boat that hooked a huge shark and was towed by it miles out towards the Mull of Kintyre. The fishermen were in trouble but were reluctant to let go of a valuable catch after a long fight. However, the Campbeltown lifeboat was called out to help the fishermen, who were unaware that there was a serious storm brewing. When the lifeboat spotted the small boat – still attached to the shark – the coxswain asked the bowman, the legendary Duncan Newlands, who was later to become one of the most famous coxswains on the west coast, to tell the fisherman that like it or not they were to be saved. It was not, according to Mr Newlands, a polite conversation. The shark, by now dead, was cast free. The storm hit on the way back to Campbeltown and the fishermen, by then desperately seasick, realised that they may have lost a shark but their lives had undoubtedly been saved.

Fortunately, these days commercial shark fishing is not sanctioned here. Shark numbers all up the west coast seem to be growing, a possible consequence of climate warming, some claim. However, as a regular traveller of this particular route, I can say that for the last few years you have had a good chance of spotting a huge black body up to 30 feet long cruising effortlessly alongside the ferry before diving deep to reappear maybe a few hundred yards away. It is a real thrill and fun to watch the reaction of tourists, and their kids, who are new to the area and who have never seen such giants of the seas close up. These are also the folk who mistake buzzards for Kintyre's golden eagles. So much so that the buzzard – a frequenter of the wooden poles that line the single-track roads around the peninsula – is known by the locals as 'the tourist eagle'.

Most folk, pedestrians and motorists, boarding the ferry for Clonaig will have missed a small memorial at Lochranza which could have given them a clue to something poignant that lies on the sea bottom, more or less on the line the ferry takes from Arran to Kintyre. The memorial commemorates the thirty-seven navy crew who died when the submarine HMS *Vandal* failed to resurface after a test dive in 1943. The death toll may have been higher, as the records fail to show if representatives of the builders, Vickers Armstrong of Barrow-in-Furness, were on board, but navy sources indicate that this would normally have been the case, as happened in the trials of the *K13* described in the previous chapter. The *Vandal* is now a war grave and the story of its loss is not one of the best remembered of Second World War disasters but is undoubtedly one of the saddest and most intriguing. The tale of the *Vandal* includes the remarkable story of a submariner who carried for fifty years feelings of guilt that he was the cause of the disaster and the death of his sea mates. It was a belief that would eventually be proved completely wrong.

But, first, there's the puzzling story of the actual sinking. In the early years of the Second World War, just as during the Great War, the submarines of the Royal Navy were again outnumbered by the massive fleet of German U-boats and the powers that be decided on a fast building programme to help us catch up with the enemy. No more K-class, thankfully.

Vandal was a product of the new spurt in manufacturing and was ordered from Vickers Armstrong in summer 1941, launched in the autumn of the next year and commissioned on 20 February 1943. Four days later it sailed from Lochranza never to be seen on the surface again.

Sailors generally are a suspicious lot and many an article has been written on their beliefs and fears. One potent notion is that changing the name of a vessel is not a bright idea and brings bad luck. The *Vandal* story underlines that. It was originally named HMS *Unbridled,* and just days before its loss its young skipper, James Bridger, had the unhappy duty of assembling his crew on the builders' yard and informing them of the name change. It caused some grumbling amongst the superstitious sailors. Some say that the idea for the name change came from Prime Minister Winston Churchill, who thought a series of subs with names beginning with 'V' would be aggressive and resonate with the word 'victory'.

The newly renamed sub headed for the Clyde to join the Third Submarine Flotilla at Holy Loch, a major base much used for trials and exercises, and a spot that was to become home to many US subs in the Cold War era. It then sailed back down the Firth for trials in deep waters off Lochranza and Inmarnock.

The newly christened *Vandal* was to have the shortest career of any sub in the navy's history. She had made her way to an anchorage just off Lochranza and the task ahead did not seem a particularly dangerous one, even though establishing the full watertightness of new subs has often caused problems. *Vandal* said goodbye to land and life early in the morning and headed towards an exercise area known to the navy as 'Quebec' and often used for calibration of submarine logs over a 'measured mile'. The crew – with an average age of twenty-four – were inexperienced, with only fifteen of them having been on a patrol previously. This was wartime and the skipper was not encouraged to be in constant radio contact. Instead the idea was that it was to be a short two or three day dress rehearsal of an actual patrol, a simulation of the real thing. The sub was expected back in the Holy Loch about teatime on 24 February, but it never arrived.

It is interesting that back in 1997 the *Herald*'s much respected then literary editor and investigative reporter, John Linklater, told his broadsheet readers that an officer who conducted acceptance trials in the Gareloch said:

I had rarely seen a U-class submarine up on trials so ably and confidently handled. The standard of the trial was extremely high in that even the greenest member of the crew appeared to have been drilled before the boat went to sea. The finished submarine was of a standard higher than we were expecting and getting even from Vickers.

This is a significant observation, for after the disaster there were years of speculation on the cause. Some of it was absurd, such as the whisper the accident had been hushed up because a Gestapo agent was on board or, even more off the wall, the idea that it was a prototype nuclear sub! But the comment on the standard of its 'build quality' and finish is important since at one stage memos flew around in the navy mentioning the suspicion of sabotage. And the possibility was taken seriously by some.

But the early stages of the investigation into what had gone wrong that February day were flawed by some bad decision-making. There was a delay in reporting that she had not made contact with base and, for that, one senior navy figure took the blame. For complex reasons, where she had actually gone down was not immediately established despite some clues. Since part of the exercise was to be deep-sea diving in the Arran Trench area of the Kilbrannan Sound, the assumption – a dangerous word – was made that this was where the accident had happened. The harbour master – some reports say the postmaster – at Lochranza said he saw a smoke candle two and a half miles off Inchmarnock. Another report talked of 'hull tapping', the sound of trapped men signalling for help, in the same area. And a spotter plane reported an oil slick in another area near Inchmarnock Island. They were important, but these clues to the scene of the disaster were ignored in an early inquiry and the loss put down to the deep dive that had been planned.

Even Winston Churchill, who had wanted the sub recovered, was told that it was impossible because of the depth of water where the sub lay – though in fact no one knew where that was. The wreck was certainly far below the waves, but one Carradale skipper told me that he had once snagged his nets on it and the depth meter indicated more than fifty fathoms! So, for years it was a mystery – though not the only one in the area.

The story of HMS *Untamed* has remarkable similarities to that of *Vandal*. Only nine weeks after the *Vandal* disappeared, *Untamed* failed to surface during a dive off Campbeltown, with the loss of all crew. It had also been Vickers built, so two new boats had now been lost in quick succession. And there had been a run of odd accidents in both Vickers yards in Barrow and on Tyneside. This was the prime cause of the suspicion of sabotage. But in the end this was not deemed to be the cause, and blame for the loss of *Untamed* was put down to the trailing log malfuctioning, which caused a sluice door to be slightly open, in turn allowing water to come in at around 2 tons a minute. This caused panic down below and some watertight compartments were not closed. Additionally, attempts to flood part of the vessel and use escape hatches failed because of the malfunctioning sluice flap.

The inquiry blamed the crew for various failings, but in hindsight this seems to be unfair since mechanical failure also played a part in the death of these submariners. A footnote to the tragedy is that a famous early 'super yacht' played a role. This was the *Shemara*, which, along with the sub, was involved in anti-submarine mortar practice. When the sub failed to surface, the yacht, a naval vessel at the time, helped locate her. After the war, the *Shemara* returned to civilian life and in the fifties was owned by Lord and Lady Docker, a flamboyant couple never far away from the gossip columns. They hosted all sorts of wild parties on the vessel and were the epitome of conspicuous consumption, sometimes at the expense of the shareholders in Lord Docker's companies. She later lay unused for around twenty years after being sold until, in spring 2014, she was refitted and relaunched, a magnificent-looking super yacht that is a reminder of a more gracious era of yachting.

The *Untamed* was salvaged and refitted as HMS *Vitality* (a somewhat ironic name, considering her history) and had an uneventful war. She was scrapped in 1946 in Troon, just across the water from the scene of her fatal sinking. The men who died in her were buried further up the Firth at Dunoon, with the exception of one sailor who was buried in Campbeltown.

The mystery of the *Vandal's* demise continued. For one

man, as mentioned earlier, the so-called 'ghost' of the *Vandal*, Larry Gaines, it meant years enduring a wrongful feeling of guilt until the wreck was found in the 1990s. Mr Gaines was a stoker on the submarine *Clyde* and became a bit of an anomaly as the man who served on the *Vandal* but never sailed on her. It came about like this: the *Clyde* was scheduled to cross the Atlantic for maintenance, but before it left four stokers, including Larry Gaines, were transferred to a new sub fitting-out in Barrow. This was the *Vandal*, though at that time it was still HMS *Unbridled*. He was twenty-one at the time, and the excitement and danger (the survival expectancy of submariners on patrol was twelve months) was a heady mixture, and young Larry and his pals made the most of their time as *Vandal* was prepared for war by drilling and practising by day. At night, the men would spend their time in the pub or out dancing.

The nickname 'ghost' in later life came about because he had been wrongly included in the list of victims. Shortly before the sub sailed for the Clyde, Gaines was stricken with an ear problem and hospitalised. Mind you, his uniform and his watch and other bits and pieces stayed in his locker. The agony of 'guilt' suffered by Gaines came about because of his wrongful belief that his absence had contributed to the sinking. His replacement on the voyage north and during the trials off Arran was a much less experienced submariner and for around sixty years Larry believed that the sailor who took over his tasks on board, which included securing the aft hatch, had not done the job properly. This was one of final checks before diving. But when, after many decades, the wreck was located in the 1990s, the aft hatch and the others were found to be closed. Larry Gaines had no hand in the tragedy and the outcome would have been the same had he been on board – with the exception, of course, that he would have been one of the victims. There had been no need to have felt guilt for all that time.

For years, no one knew where exactly the wreck lay, but half a century later fishermen in the Kilbrannan Sound began to report nets snagging on an object a mere mile and a half from Lochranza harbour. This was some 20 miles from the the original search area. When it was finally found in 1994 by the navy, much of the credit was owed to a remarkable man called Sandy Young, who used his skill in detective work – he had been in the London police and at one time had had his own agency – to analyse all available clues and to come up with an answer that made sense.

But speculation continued and will continue about the exact cause of the accident. Nine years after the navy had confirmed the location of the object snagging the nets, a 2003 expedition involving Sandy Young and Brian Thomas of the Submariners Association dived into the dark waters of the Kilbrannan Sound, their task to make a positive identification. Conditions underwater were extremely difficult and it required bravery and persistence to get the job done.

On day one of the expedition, a diver called Leigh Bishop found part of the conning tower with the nameplate *Vandal*. Further examination showed that indeed the aft hatch had played no part in the disaster – so there was no doubt that poor Larry Gaines had spent years worrying unnecessarily. The tips of the propeller were badly damaged, presumably by the young skipper desperately trying to power his vessel back to the surface. Oddly, mooring ropes on the deck were seen neatly stowed and this indicated to experts that the trouble had begun on the surface, as on a planned dive they would have been taken inboard.

So, what did happen? It's true that other subs had sunk owing to trouble in getting back inboard towed logs, which are used to track speed and other navigational information, and log tests were part of the *Vandal* trials. But as to what actually happened on that fateful day, it must all remain as speculation. There was no obvious cause that could be identified by the divers who found the wreck and we may never know what really happened.

At the end of the 2003 diving expedition, Sandy Young and representatives of the Submariners Association and the divers and diving crews involved visited the *Vandal* memorial on Inchmarnock Island. Prayers were said and a toast drunk to the lost crew and to those submariners still on patrol around the world. An emotional moment.

These days, many pass by the exact spot where the *Vandal* lies, though most are unaware of it. The much busier ferry journey from Ardrossan to Brodick on Arran's east coast also sails waters with a deadly history and much greater loss of life in the Second World War. In the spring of 1943 a British aircraft carrier, HMS *Dasher*, exploded while on exercise between Ayrshire and the island, killing 389 of the 528 on board – a horrific death toll.

Amazingly, this wartime disaster is little known even today, despite the huge loss of life. At the time the government made attempts, which to a certain extent succeeded, to prevent the public hearing about the explosion and the disaster. They feared that the news would be a particularly powerful blow to morale, with the war still at its height. There was also another more reprehensible reason, which we'll come to, to keep what happened on a March day off Arran from the prying eyes of the public, some of whom had watched the *Dasher* in action in the Firth as its pilots practised take-off and landings a few miles from their front doors. Many on Arran heard the massive fatal explosion, but the local press was largely silenced by the government. Rescue-boat crews were warned not to talk about what they had seen and even the survivors were sent on a fortnight's leave, with the instructions that they were not to talk about the disaster. A tall order, you would think. Today men and women involved in such a disaster would receive professional help from trauma specialists, but around seventy years ago this was not even given a thought. Go home and forget it, said the navy. It is interesting to note, though, that reflecting the sort of mistakes that happen during war, some national newspapers reported the disaster while readers of the local press were denied knowledge of an incident on their doorstep. The second reason for secrecy was a rather nasty one – the government did not want to damage relations with its American allies.

The reason for this lies in the early history of the *Dasher*. It was never intended to be an aircraft carrier and started life as a merchantman originally named *Rio de Janeiro* and built in the US. But the pressure of the war at sea meant that the Royal Navy needed escort carriers quickly, so, a class of converted American merchantmen was assembled. At the time this made a lot of sense since purpose-built carriers took a long time to build. But a conversion is seldom as successful as a new build, and maybe that is a clue to why the *Dasher* exploded.

The *Rio de Janeiro* was renamed HMS *Dasher* in July 1942 after conversion in a New Jersey shipyard. All her commercial top-deck overworks had been swept away and a long wooden flight deck added, and a small bridge and flight-control tower created on the starboard side. At around 8,000 tons she was not a particularly impressive sight, but she could carry fifteen aircraft, a mixture of an American Grumman type, Sea Hurricane fighters and that trusty old warhorse, the Fairey Swordfish. *Dasher* was to have a short life.

After the alterations, she took part, along with a sister ship, HMS *Biter*, in Operation Torch in the Mediterranean before sailing for the Clyde in early 1943. She successfully escorted one convoy from Scotland, but her next sortie was cut short by engine trouble and she returned to the Clyde area, where she was seen steaming up and down off Arran, training pilots. It was at this point she was blasted apart by an internal explosion and sank beneath the waves and into relative obscurity for years, much to the distress of the victims' families, who were angered by the cover-up.

The credit for salvaging the story of the *Dasher* to a large extent belongs to a remarkable Ayrshire couple, John and Noreen Steele, who have written several books on the disaster and extensively researched the explosion and the aftermath, including the controversial topic of what happened to the bodies. But there still remain plenty of unsolved mysteries and speculative theories surrounding one of the most remarkable stories in the Royal Navy's history.

Back in 1943, the nearness to Arran and Ayrshire meant that there was a swift response by rescue craft from Brodick, Lamlash, Ardrossan and Greenock. Many of those who escaped the ship died from burns when fuel caught fire in the water; others died of hypothermia. Wild reports circulated that it had been torpedoed or hit by a mine, both ideas that seemed to have little chance of being accurate, as the Firth of Clyde at the time was held to be U-boat free and the waters were swept successfully by mine hunters. Another explanation put forward was that an aircraft had crashed on landing and fuel had ignited, causing the explosion, but no one onshore had seen such a thing happen and neither had any of the survivors. A more likely reason was bad design inherent in the conversion.

In its short life *Dasher* emitted an almost constant smell of petrol. In any carrier some smells from oil leaks and aviation fuel-storage tanks is to be expected. But the chatter, admittedly unscientific, about petrol fumes on the *Dasher* highlighted, in retrospect, something out of the ordinary. Was it a result of botched design work on the conversion of a merchantman to a carrier? It is a substantive theory. In 2011, those dedicated and painstaking researchers John and Noreen Steele in their book *The American Connection to the Sinking of HMS Dasher* seemed to confirm such a theory. In it they revealed that the long-forgotten Board of Inquiry found the explosion most likely occurred in the main petrol compartment 'and was most likely ignited by a man smoking in the shaft tunnel or someone dropping a cigarette down from the mess deck above'. In view of this it is perhaps easier to understand the attempted gagging of the news of the death of the *Dasher*. It is not a story the navy can be proud of. Britain officially blamed the Americans for design faults in the *Dasher*, something the builders rejected. In the Americans' favour it can be pointed out that the navy training of crews on the converted merchantmen was, after investigation, labelled as being poor. And afterwards both navies adopted new procedures on handling petrol on carriers. Maybe, too, the navy should itself have done something about that smell of petrol. It was clearly a matter of concern to those serving on the ship, but, of course, in times of war the rules can be very different. With an enemy knocking at the door, the focus has to be on keeping all available military resources in fighting condition.

It is a shocking story. There is, however, another aspect of the tragedy of the *Dasher* that resonates to this day. What happened to the bodies? Only twelve of the bodies were buried with full military honours in Ardrossan cemetery. Yet for weeks after the explosion bodies continued to be washed ashore. What happened to the hundreds of other victims? All this prompted speculation about a mass grave, something that is of immense importance to the families of the dead. These days, the bereaved are said to desperately seek 'closure' and for that you need a grave and the full story of what happened to your loved one. This is something that has not happened for the relatives of those who died on *Dasher*.

Enter John Steele again. He has spent years on all aspects of the *Dasher* story, interviewing many people and drilling into the navy records. In May 2010, his research pointed to the existence of a mass grave and culminated in an approach to Dr Tony Pollard, director of Battlefield Archaeology at Glasgow University, who found, after a low-level radar examination of a possible area of Ardrossan cemetery, that, 'This survey does not rule out the possibility that there may be a large pit containing numerous bodies without coffins.' Of course, neither does it rule it in. Mr Steele is still anxious for the truth on this part of the *Dasher* saga to be established, and it may yet happen as a result of further investigation. Let's hope so.

One further intriguing aspect of the *Dasher* story is its connection with Operation Mincemeat in 1943, and, again, the indefatigable John Steele plays a major role in this story. This operation was a wartime plan to fool German intelligence into thinking the Allies were planning attacks on Greece when, in fact, the intended target was Sicily. Winston Churchill was an early sceptic about the plan to drop the body of a 'Major Martin' from a submarine into the sea near Huelva, Spain, where it would be washed up and the body searched. 'Major Martin' was to have a briefcase chained to his arm containing fake documents that indicated that the Allies were about to launch a major attack on Greece. The body was to be in Royal Marine uniform and to appear to have died from drowning.

Great care went into the deception in order that those who found the body would have no doubt that it was genuine. The wartime prime minister did not have much faith in this plan and is said to have remarked that 'anyone but a bloody fool would know it was Sicily'. He was wide of the mark, as the plan, mainly devised by Lt Commander Ewan Montagu, was so successful that when Spanish Intelligence handed the body and its 'secret documents' to the Germans they swallowed it whole. As Churchill was told in a message sent to him later: 'Mincemeat swallowed rod, line and sinker.' General Alfred Jodl, head of the German supreme command operations, boasted openly, 'You can forget about Sicily. We know it is Greece.'

Modern historians consider this prime example of the dark arts of deception as dreamt up by Ewan Montagu and British Intelligence as a major factor in the success of the invasion of Sicily. Operation Husky, as the invasion was codenamed, went more smoothly than anyone could have hoped. It must have been a great help to our forces that the enemy thought the actions were to happen 500 miles away from actual landings! Such a wonderful story was a natural for a film and ten years later it became one: *The Man Who*

Never Was. This was based on a book of the same name by Ewan Montagu, which was, as you might expect from a man with his background, an interesting confection of fact and fiction. Maybe, too, there was an intention not to let all the truths out of the bag. The film had the big-name treatment, starring Clifton Webb, Gloria Grahame and Robert Flemyng, and was a box office and critical hit, with the screenplay by Nigel Balchin winning a BAFTA in 1956.

But this version of Operation Mincemeat triggered another mystery that was not to be solved beyond reasonable doubt for more than sixty years. Who took the role of Major Martin, who was dumped into the sea? For years, the story went that the body of a homeless Welshman called Glyndwr Michael was used. But in 2003 a former policeman, Colin Gribbon, produced research, which was turned into a documentary, claiming that the body was a victim of the *Dasher* explosion, a sailor called Tom Martin. The next year there was a dramatic twist to the tale at a memorial service to those who died off Arran – held on board the current HMS *Dasher*, a navy patrol vessel – when an answer to the mystery emerged. Lt Commander Mark Hill named John Melville, another member of the *Dasher* crew, as the man who stood in for the man who never was, Major William Martin of the Royal Marines. John Melville was described as 'a man who most certainly was' and his daughter told *The Scotsman*: 'I feel very honoured if my father saved thousands of Allied lives.'

But there is an alternative theory. When researching for his book *Operation Mincemeat: Death, Deception and the Mediterranean D-Day*, Professor Denis Smyth of Toronto University came across a secret memo by Ewan Montagu that seems to confirm that the body of the Welshman was used. Will anyone every really know? Like John Steele, I go with the Melville theory. Anyone looking at the mystery might give a thought to the fact that Montagu was a master of deceit and deception. Would he have decided to fool his own side with the Glyndwr Michael story because the elite of the British high command might not have liked the idea of 'stealing' a body that should have been in a war grave? You could also give a thought to the fact that the sub, the *Seraph*, sailed from the Clyde on its long journey to the coast of Spain and one of the greatest deceptions in military and naval history, and that its skipper, Bill Jewell, is adamant that the body of a man that some called a tramp and a drunk would not have been used. Is it not more likely that the Germans would have been fooled by a body that had all the hallmarks of the military that they would have expected to see? And having gone to so much effort to fool the Germans, it seems implausible that British Intelligence would have risked the failure of the entire operation by using a body that was clearly not of a military bearing.

5

SKILL AND HEROISM OFF 'SPOON ISLAND'

The lucky folk who live in and around the lovely village of Southend at the southern tip of the Kintyre peninsula – and the equally lucky holiday-makers who flock there in the summer to play golf, swim, walk the beaches or search out the abundant wildlife – are spoiled for choice when it comes to spectacular views. As you stand on the beach at Dunaverty Bay there is a 360-degree panorama of interest. To the west, a few miles across a channel of fast-flowing currents and dangerous waves, lashed up in winter by frequent gales, lies Ireland. So near – around 13 miles away – are the gently sloping hills of the island that in the early part of the twentieth century the crossing began to challenge long-distance swimmers as a change from ploughing from Dover, far to the south, to the shores of France.

On a summer's day, draw your eye back from the pleasure of watching clouds and sun speckle the green island with alternate light and darkness, and your view changes dramatically. Now the high cliffs of the Mull of Kintyre dominate the scenery, towering over the breaking surf.

Inland lies some of the best agricultural land in Scotland, a fine place to farm and only held back from being massively profitable by its distance from the markets of the crowded Lowlands. Standing on the beach, turn your back on the sea and you can watch sportsmen and women enjoy the challenge of a round of golf on the pleasant links of Dunaverty, a place that produced perhaps Scotland's finest female golfer, Belle Robertson. Swivel a little further to your right and at the end of the beautiful curve of the bay lies the ruins of the Dunaverty lifeboat station, some derelict buildings and the remains of a steep slipway down which lifeboat and lifeboatmen were hurled to get to sea in a huge splash of breaking water on another mission of mercy.

Beyond the site of the lifeboat station lies the tip of Arran, and from there islanders looked over the Firth of Clyde to Sanda, and what they saw created a local nickname. Arran folk called it 'Spoon Island' because of its shape viewed from their shores. Just off the Mull of Kintyre, the rocks of Sanda and Sheep Island are a danger to shipping passing under the cliffs of the mainland en route to Ireland or bound for the wild waters of the Atlantic and distant ports, as are other small islands, numerous reefs and the infamous Paterson's Rock. Navigation around here is also complicated by strong currents as the Firth of Clyde, the Irish Sea and the great Atlantic Ocean mingle. Indeed, even on what you might expect to be a calm summer's day, huge rollers come in from the Atlantic to hammer Westport Beach near Machrihanish and provide some good cold-water surfing for hardy souls on boards or kayaks.

Since 1869, there has been a lighthouse on Sanda, but, despite this, vessels keep hitting the island. Two of Scotland's most illustrious divers and wreck explorers, Ian

61

Crawford and Peter Moir, have written extensively and expertly on the vessels lying under Scotland's cruel seas. Their *Argyll Shipwrecks* is particularly good on the area around Sanda. The most important wreck in the area is the American Liberty ship the *Byron Darnton,* which ran aground on 16 March 1946. It was one of hundreds of such no-frills freighters built during the war to facilitate moving supplies to Europe from the US at a time when German U-boats were hunting in packs and sinking merchant vessels almost at will. The *Byron Darnton* survived the war but not a voyage back from the Clyde to the States.

It is by far the most famous of the wrecks of Sanda, though there have been many other marine tragedies in the area, especially around the Boiler Reef, which claimed both *Byron Darnton* and the *Hereford Express* in relatively recent times. The lifeboat station was opened at Dunaverty, just across from the island on the mainland, more than a hundred years ago and there have been many tales of bravery and disasters in the years since – too many to describe in detail, though the wrecks that are left now make it a paradise for sub-aqua enthusiasts. One of the most noteworthy of the earliest sinkings was the sailing vessel the *Perica,* which was dismasted in a storm and driven onto the rocks. Five people lost their lives, but the lighthouse keepers and a local man who farmed on the tiny island at the time rescued others, including the skipper, in remarkable fashion. The grounding occurred on New Year's Day 1865 (surprising how often Christmas and New Year are times of tragedies involving ships, trains or planes). The wooden barque was taking rum and sugar to Greenock. Some of the crew drowned trying to get to shore by hanging onto bits of drifting wreckage. But as the day progressed, the huge seas eased a little and rescuers managed to take to the water in a skiff that had been dragged across the island to the site of the disaster and saved many of the crew.

The *Hereford Express* was a motor vessel of around 200 tons and had the distinction of going aground twice in a few hours in the autumn of 1970. She was en route from Londonderry to Glasgow when she ran aground near the Mull of Kintyre. A German ship, MV *Hope Island,* was in the vicinity and she tried to tow the damaged ship to safety, but the towline broke several times and the vessel drifted onto the Boiler Reef on Sanda. The crew managed to get ashore safely. Not so lucky were the 250 cattle that made up the ship's cargo. An RSPCA inspector was able to board the vessel and humanely kill the cattle just as the ship went down. Nearby is another wreck – that of a salvage vessel that sank when involved in operations on the wreck of the *Byron Darnton.* This is certainly a very busy area for wrecks.

The tale of the rescue of fifty-four passengers and crew (and a puppy) from the *Byron Darnton* is one of the most dramatic accounts of a lifeboat rescue ever told. It has been immortalised in countless newspaper articles, in books and on radio. By far the best rendering of the tale is in *Rescue Call,* published by Kaye and Ward in 1967. The author is one of Scotland's best-known writers, Angus MacVicar, and no one was better equipped to tell this story. MacVicar wrote more than fifty books, ranging from adventure and sci-fi stories for a young audience to a series of witty and highly acclaimed personal memoirs. In addition, he stayed for years in sight of Sanda, just three miles across the water from his home in Southend. He had an adventurous Second World War, being mentioned in dispatches, and was auxiliary coastguard and member of the Southend Life-Saving apparatus crew. And if that was not enough, he was a friend of Duncan Newlands of Campbeltown, one of the most famous and skilled coxswains in the British lifeboat service.

Rescue Call is an enthralling history of the lifeboats that is as meticulous in detail as it is well written. It is packed with stories of sea rescues, all compelling reading, but for a Scot the most intriguing is the rescue of passengers and crew of the *Byron Darnton*. The fifty-four saved is a record for the Campbeltown lifeboat station. Before he left Scotland to return to the US, the master of the *Byron Darnton*, Robert King, wrote a remarkable letter to coxswain Duncan Newlands:

On behalf of the crew of the Byron Darnton, as well as the officers and passengers and myself, I want to try to express our gratitude. Never in all my experience as a ship's captain have I seen nobler men or more capable. The manner in which you and your crew attacked the most trying and difficult task of rescuing all of us in the terrific gale and heavy seas that were in existence at that time is beyond my ability to describe. I, too, want to thank you for your very efficient ability on our shore-bound voyage from the ship, especially when the motor of the boat gave out and you were forced to hoist a sail. The most I can say is thank you. God bless you and may you continue to be the example of a seaman that you really are.

That says it all about the sort of men Duncan Newlands and his crew were. On 16 March 1946, a storm cone was hoisted on the signalling mast at Campbeltown quay. The cone was part of a primitive system for warning seafarers about deteriorating weather in the days before electronic gizmos took over, even on the smallest of yachts. In 1946, ships still took to the seas without even the benefit of radio-telephones. Remarkable as it seems today, the lifeboat used in the rescue, as well as not having RT communications also did not have a masthead signal lamp or that necessity, a powerful searchlight, to help locate those in distress. It was almost midnight on the Saturday when the lifeboat, the *Duke of Connaught,* sailed out of Campbeltown Loch past Davaar Island and steered out into the Kilbrannan Sound, heading for Sanda off the Mull of Kintyre. The first news of trouble had come from a phone call to Campbeltown (known to its denizens and neighbours as 'the Wee Toon') shortly after 11 p.m. Immediately, the shore signalman fired the traditional maroons to attract the crew.

Normally a Watson-class lifeboat like the 45-foot *Duke of Connaught* carried a crew of eight, but this dark night, with fog and gales and the promise of trouble ahead, the wily Duncan Newlands thought an extra man would help and a crew of nine mustered: Newlands himself, with Duncan Black as the bowman and second mechanic, Duncan MacLean, Archie MacKay, James Lang, Willie Blair, Sam Brodie, Danny McAulay and J.H. Lister as the first mechanic. The 'old *Duke*' was standing in as a reserve, as the regular boat was away undergoing an overhaul. And though a wonderful seagoing vessel, she had a bit of a reputation for being temperamental and there was a record of the engine acting up. The seas were heavy and dangerous, but Southend was reached without incident.

There, coxswain Newlands got in touch with the coastguards using a hand lamp and Morse code. Newlands knew the danger of the Boiler Reef well and suspected that was where the vessel had gone aground. The coastguards also thought this might be the scene of the disaster and that the

distress rockets seen by them had been fired in that area. Off
Sanda, the seas were heavy and Duncan Newlands told his
friend Angus MacVicar that 'it was darker than a whale's
belly'. In spite of the poor visibility, the lifeboatmen spotted
lights inshore below the lighthouse. Their worst fears were
confirmed when they realised the lights were shining from
inside the Boiler Reef. Newland used the klaxon and the
hand lamp – which was acting up because of battery trouble
– to try to attract attention. No flare or acknowledgement
that they had been spotted came to the lifeboat's attention.

Meanwhile, as the crew of the *Duke* tried everything they
knew to attract anyone aboard the *Darnton*, the storm
worsened. Eventually it occurred to coxswain and crew that
perhaps there was no sign of life because the lighthouse
keepers had rescued the occupants of the *Byron Darnton*.
Certainly she seemed a 'dead and empty' ship, as Duncan
Newlands put it. And, anyway, at that stage of the tide it
would have been impossible to go inside the reef and alongside the ship. In addition, at that time the safety of the lifeboat itself was at risk. The only hope was daylight and high
water, so the old *Duke* headed for the only place where it
might get some relief from the storm, a little harbour on the
north side of the island. There, too, they could get some
information from Sandy Russell and his son Jim, who
farmed on the island. Naturally, Duncan Newlands, who
knew the coast, in the old cliché, like the back of his hand,
also knew Sandy and Jim well.

Newlands anchored offshore to await daylight, as snow
now mixed with the strong winds. At 4 a.m., almost five
hours after they had left base, there was no sign of Sandy
and Jim, whose farmhouse was a bit back from the harbour.
The crew began to wonder if the farmers were across at the

lighthouse with survivors. With no radio-telephone or any other communication, the crew were in limbo. What if the passengers and crew were still on the ship? This thought was at the forefront of the minds of Duncan Newlands and his crew. They itched to get back to the wreck and the mood was sombre. Shortly before dawn, and after some hot soup, the anchor was hauled and the lifeboat headed out again into the full gale. The seas were ferocious and one giant wave damaged the rudder, snapping off steel pins like matchsticks. This was no place to be with dicky steering. They had to return to the tiny harbour, where it took six lines to hold the lifeboat to the jetty, to fit an emergency tiller.

This time Jim Russell and his cousin John Thomson, who was on the farm at the time, heard the klaxon and came down to the jetty with shocking news – no one had been taken off the *Byron Darnton*. Fifty-four lives were still at risk. It was surmised that when the lifeboat had arrived at the wreck in the pitch dark and at the height of the storm, those aboard had neither heard the klaxon nor seen the faint light of the hand lamp. There was breaches buoy equipment at the lighthouse and five of the lifeboat crew went ashore to cross the island on foot, in the company of Jim Russell and John Thomson. It was not long before they were back, bearing bad news. At the lighthouse, one of the keepers had semaphored the ship indicating the idea was to fire a line to it and affect a breeches buoy rescue. Captain King thought this was too dangerous, especially for the female passengers. This did not exactly please the lifeboatmen, but Duncan Newlands asked Jim Russell, because of his local knowledge, to come and help pilot the *Duke* in past the reef and alongside the ship in another rescue attempt. John

Thomson also bravely agreed to join them. As a hint of what was to come, the engine initially refused to start and it took much cranking and effort to remove water that had come in by way of the exhausts.

By now, it was around lunchtime on the Sunday and at last in full daylight they got a good look at the stranded Liberty ship. She was in immediate danger of breaking in two and sinking. As all aboard the vessel, fast on the reef, had sheltered from the waves, the radio officer had been sending messages throughout the night asking for assistance. These messages were picked up at Portpatrick radio station and rebroadcast. Tugs were delayed by the ferocity of the storm and arrived too late. The Portpatrick and Girvan lifeboats also put to sea but were beaten back by the storm and unable to find the ship. Meantime, with all this other rescue activity going on, the crew of the *Duke of Connaught* remained completely in the dark about what was happening around them.

During the night, awaiting rescue, the crew and passengers kept calm, but later Captain King told of the pounding the stricken vessel was taking and that he knew it was only a matter of time until it broke apart. And at around midday there was nothing to do other than to give the order to abandon ship as it broke up under him. It was an American ship bound for New York and there was a touch of Hollywood in what happened next. Captain King had hardly finished his announcement when he caught sight of the Campbeltown lifeboat riding to the rescue. But there was no easy solution. A direct run inside the reef was impossible, but local knowledge came into play and Jim Russell mentioned he knew of a narrow passage between sharp rocks in behind the stern of the ship. It was a dangerous place to take a lifeboat, but there seemed no alternative. Any indecision was swept away as the lifeboatmen watched the cargo vessel start to break up before their eyes. Newlands and his men made their move.

Good luck kept the engine running and the emergency tiller did its bit. Captain King had his lifeboats lowered, ropes were thrown and ships' boats were hauled towards the rescuers and the women pulled aboard. Meanwhile, men clambered desperately down ropes into a lifeboat that acted as a buffer between the old *Duke* and the breaking wreck. One man arrived on the lifeboat with a Husky puppy wrapped in his coat. The adrenalin flowed as lifeboatmen reached into the boiling surf and heaved the dead weight of survivors from the water with what seemed like superhuman strength. With fifty of the passengers and crew aboard, it is said that Duncan Newlands asked, 'Any more to come?' He was told four were still aboard, getting a case of whisky for their rescuers. At the last possible moment they appeared and Duncan Newlands told them not to drop the whisky case onto the lifeboat, in case it caused damage, and suggested instead that it was dropped in the water. The coxswain – a lifelong teetotaller and a fan of ginger wine – made an apparent effort to hook it in on board with a boathook, but the case floated away and was never seen again. It was a nice gesture by Captain King, but there were more important matters now to hand.

In behind the reef and the wreck, it was impossible to turn and the lifeboat had to be backed out, no mean feat of seamanship, but it was accomplished despite a few scrapes. The operation had been made all the more difficult by the fact that the lifeboat was now deeper in the water with the weight of fifty-four survivors, something that was to cause trouble in the next stage of the rescue.

The folk plucked from likely death on Boiler Reef were an interesting crowd –thirty-nine crew members and fifteen passengers. The freighter was in ballast and was heading from Copenhagen to Gourock and then back out into the Atlantic, bound for New York. Among the passengers were seven young Norwegian girls who had won scholarships to universities in the US. There was also a GI bride and a female officer who had fought for the Danish underground. There were four male Norwegians aboard. And there was the puppy carried ashore, though it did not add too much additional weight.

Heading back to Campbeltown, the *Duke* was against a strong tide and the seas, though moderating, were still difficult. Even under engine power the lifeboat, low in the water, was travelling slowly. But worse was to come. The temperamental engine, which up to that point had been struggling, decided to have another tantrum and stopped completely. Before this had happened an attempt was made to set a jib sail, but the American sailors were traumatised and unable to help, so it was deemed wiser to try to proceed on lugsail alone: not much canvas for a heavily laden vessel.

The trouble was that water had entered the engine via the exhaust pipes, which were being submerged in the heavy seas at times. The two mechanics on board worked hard to try to solve the problem, but as if the lifeboat was not in enough danger, the lugsail then burst and left the boat virtually powerless. Duncan Newlands told Angus MacVicar that Captain King thought 'we have had it now', but the Campbeltown man was not beaten yet. As the remains of the lugsail were lowered, all the hard work on the engine paid off. The exhausts were blocked and water cranked out of the engine and, astonishingly, it came back to life. In

Rescue Call Angus MacVicar wrote that Newlands was struck by the courage and calm of the women particularly. And with the engine working, if not fully, the coxswain ordered a rum ration to be passed round. He contented himself with his usual tipple of ginger wine. Semaphore signals were sent to the lighthouse on Davaar Island and ambulances met the *Duke* at the Campbeltown quayside. The sick were taken to hospital and others to hotels for hot baths and food.

All this was not without cost and the Shipwrecked Fishermen and Mariners' Royal Benevolent Society, which had been funded by donations from local people, paid out around £500. Sadly, the one sour note in this epic tale of lifeboat rescue was that it was reported at the time that the owners of the *Byron Darnton* gave no cash to the RNLI itself.

On a happier note, the husky puppy Suji spent two days in Campbeltown jail before being sent away to quarantine. It was not what you would call a tough stretch in the nick – it was said that while behind bars the police found that Suji was 'partial to milk and sweeties'.

Two modern tragedies are also burned into the folk memories of Argyll – the loss of the Carradale fishing vessel *Antares*, dealt with later in this book, and the sinking of the motor yacht *Quesada*.

In this invented journey round Scotland, it would be remiss to leave the Campbeltown area without telling the story of one of the Wee Toon's most tragic events, the loss of the *Quesada* in 1966 in which eight lost their lives. One of the most prolific chroniclers of the history of the area is Freddie Gillies of Gigha. These days, Freddie plies his trade as a ferry master for CalMac, but he began as 'a youngster at the fishing', as they say on the west coast, many years ago. Profitable voyages out into the Kilbrannan Sound and around the Mull of Kintyre, and up the west coast to the Minch followed, as well as to Southern Ireland and the waters around the Isle of Man. Adventurous times, but although Freddie clearly has the sea in his blood, somehow or other it got mixed with printers' ink. He left the fishing to go into journalism, first with his local paper, the *Campbeltown Courier* (and as a stringer for the national press), and then in the English Midlands, where he made quite a name for himself and got material for a readable book on journalism in the hot-metal days. He had fun as a scribbler before giving in to the lure of salt water and returning to the sea on the small car ferries so popular in the area. He is an author of a number of informative and entertaining books on many aspects of Kintyre life. He is also a publisher. Freddie is good company and an accomplished raconteur and it was he who first put me on the trail of what happened to the *Quesada* and the devastating effect that it had on his home town.

It all began cheerfully enough. The 58-foot-long *Quesada* was a good-looking vessel but a bit of a veteran when she went down, having been built in 1938 in Southampton. When operating out of Campbeltown, she had some success as a pleasure cruiser taking small groups on outings. There was not much to indicate that soon eight people were to lose their lives on her; though, despite a successful career in the West Highlands, her previous owner had had some doubts about her handling.

The voyage that was to end in drama had been organised by John Paterson, son of a local garage owner. It was not an official works outing, though ten of the passengers worked in the garage. Young John paid around £35 to the owner and his mates chipped in £2 10s each for the trip. The Campbeltown folk were in good humour and looking forward to a day away from the routine when their charter vessel sailed at 7.45 a.m. on Sunday, 22 May 1966. The original idea had been to sail to Northern Ireland, but the waters off the Mull, which would have to be navigated, are at the best of times notorious for dangerous tides and high seas.

It was sensible to have a rethink and everyone agreed that a trip to more sheltered waters was a good idea, especially having heard the 5.45 a.m. weather forecast: 'There are warnings of gales in Lundy, Irish Sea, Fastnet and Malin. Malin wind mainly south-westerly force 6 to gale force 8 veering north-westerly. Rain followed by showers. Visibility moderate becoming good.' When out of Campbeltown Loch and abreast of Davaar Island, a turn to port, heading for Lochranza on Arran, was made. On board were John McMillan, owner and skipper, who was assisted by the other crew member, Archie Stewart, a vastly experienced retired fisherman who knew the proposed route intimately. The crew had three friends aboard – a radio mechanic, a marine engineer and a young boy. They also assisted the skipper from time to time. Reaching Lochranza was relatively easy, though there was perhaps a hint of trouble ahead when a minor fault in one of the twin engines had to be repaired. Apart from that, all was well, aside from some of the passengers, who were seasick.

There was a coffee stop on the island and it was agreed that the *Quesada* would sail to the popular holiday resort of Rothesay via the Kyles of Bute, one of the most scenic sea routes in all Scotland. Rothesay was achieved at 2.30 p.m. and the passengers got a couple of hours or so ashore and some took advantage of this to have a meal in the Lorne Hotel. Then it was time to head back home, again through the Kyles to Tighnabruaich, where there was more time ashore and another hotel visit. On the way back all was well until the charter was passing Skipness, where the wind got up. A few miles down the Sound at Carradale the wind started to really make itself felt. On the run from the Cruban buoy off Carradale beach to Campbeltown, it was reaching gale force 8 from the north-west. The veteran Archie Stewart took the wheel, and despite the conditions, it was said he had no fear for the safety of his passengers. The vessel had some shelter from a weather shore, where the hills were protecting the vessel from the worst of the wind, and it was said at a subsequent inquiry that she was well handled, though the wind introduced a list. Mr Stewart chose, because of the prevailing conditions, to pass outside the Otterard Rock buoy when approaching Campbeltown Loch.

Suddenly, a quarter-mile north of Davaar lighthouse, when Archie Stewart was opening up the guiding lights into the loch, he found his vessel would not take starboard helm and almost at the same moment the port engine failed. There was no easy way into the calm waters of the loch now and, as John McMillan and Jack McCallum went to the engine room to confirm the port engine had indeed stopped, the helmsman was told to 'keep her head to the wind', an impossible command in a gale and with only one engine. A watcher onshore saw the *Quesada* and he thought that at the time she was still under power and not drifting, but he soon lost sight of her behind the island. Soon, the starboard engine also stopped and the vessel was down by the stern and drifting.

A good marine radio receiver and transmitter was on

board, though it had only been used to listen to weather reports. Now it was in serious action – a Mayday was sent out at 12.45 a.m. on the Monday morning. It seems, too, that some flares were sent up when the vessel was near Davaar, but these were not seen in Campbeltown because of the bulk of the island.

At this time the life-saving equipment was issued and the subsequent inquiry found that it was unclear how many life jackets were on board, but that not everyone had one. The report said:

> *Jack McCallum had been seen to have a lifebuoy but when his body was recovered later a life jacket was nearby. It is not certain if John McMillan had one. Archibald Stewart did not have one, but this appears to have been by choice [many fishermen at that time had an aversion to such things]. There was also a life raft on board but the three or four who went overboard with it were lost. The experienced helmsman Stewart advised all who could to stick to the boat, which was good advice. It was a nightmare out on the water, but onshore there was also real concern. Neil Paterson had handled the ship on a trip to Northern Ireland and was unhappy about the way she behaved. He also felt that there was a lack of power and that she would be blown onto the Arran shore in such a gale.*

Mr Paterson was seriously worried about the whereabouts of the *Quesada*. He foraged around for news since little had been heard of her after the departure from Rothesay. Also concerned during a night almost as wild ashore as out at sea was Jack Wareham, who was also enquiring about the ship. Mr Paterson got him to contact the coastguard at Southend and they sent a signal to colleagues at Portpatrick, who broadcast, looking for information on the ship. The immediate result was negative. The court of inquiry found that there was a conflict of evidence between Mr Paterson, who lost his only son, and lifeboat officials.

All this was in the future, but as the clock ticked the concern among those who knew folk on the excursion grew. The brother of the owner was up and down the Carradale road looking for the ship more than once, as were others. These groups met up on the road about three miles from Campbeltown and reported that the *Quesada* was on course. This was before any engine trouble. In a night of confusion and anxiety, the secretary of the Campbeltown branch of the RNLI was making his way to the lifeboat station when he saw a flare south of Davaar, and at 1 a.m. maroons were fired calling the lifeboat crew. Only twelve minutes later the lifeboat sailed, a remarkable feat since some crew members had to be collected by car. The inquiry found that 'the activities of the coastguard stations involved and the lifeboat officials were in accordance with the best traditions of both services and deserving of the highest commendations'. There was an acerbic footnote, observing 'one wonders why the Southend coastguard station is not more fully equipped'.

But the most remarkable event in the *Quesada* story is the efforts of the Campbeltown fishermen to save life. It is worth recording the words in the official inquiry report:

The greatest part in the rescue operations was by certain Campbeltown fishermen. Neil Speed, owner of the fishing boat Moira, *Archibald Galbraith, Duncan McArthur, Sweeney Copping, Norman Thomson and Campbell Stewart, with James Meenan, owner of the fishing boat* Regina Maris. *These men were sleeping, or preparing to sleep, aboard over Sunday night, preparatory to going out on the Monday morning. Within a few minutes of the flare being seen south of Davaar, these men were off in the* Moira *on a mission of rescue. Neil Speed was in command of his own boat, ably assisted by James Meenan, who directed operations. On the way out of the loch, lengths of rope were cut in preparation of rescue work. The skill, cool courage, intelligence and character shown by these men, which resulted in the saving of ten lives in a full gale, from the sinking vessel, with spindrift making vision impossible, is deserving of the highest praise and commendation. Neil Speed's skilful handling of the* Moira *alongside the sinking* Quesada, *with James Meenan's direction of operation, are in the highest and best traditions of the sea.*

This was the legal assessment of what happened that night and the rescue of ten people. The most accomplished writer of fiction, surrounded by thesauruses and dictionaries, whisky to hand, could not have told it better. You could not have made it up. This was real-life heroism more powerful than any fictional adventure story.

The *Moira* had returned to Campbeltown with ten survivors, but when they were safely ashore it went out again and continued the search until the following afternoon, along with the lifeboat and other local fishing boats: *Regina Maris, Mary McLean, Golden Hind, Little Flower, Boy Danny* and *Regina.* No more survivors were found, though the life raft and a little dinghy that had been on board were collected, along with bits of debris from the *Quesada,* which now lay on the sea bottom. Incidentally, there was one cheery touch amid the tragedy – 'Baldy' Stewart, a real Campbeltown character, took his wee terrier dog safely off *Quesada* with him.

Like many accidents, it cannot be established what one thing caused the disaster: it was a combination of circumstances, weather and mechanical failure. The inquiry came up with various sensible recommendations. On the question of whether *Quesada* was seaworthy in all respects, it was found that it did not have the necessary life-saving appliances as required by law, and notices were not displayed showing what equipment was available and how to use it. There were other criticisms on deck openings, strength of doorways and so on. But it should be remembered that the tragedy happened in times when health-and-safety regulations were not imposed as stringently.

The memory of those who lost their lives will live on, as will the efforts of the fishermen of Campbeltown in saving ten of the eighteen who set sail for a pleasant day out one Sunday morning in 1966.

6

THE LIFEBOAT HEROES OF
THE WILD WEST COAST

There is something in the Argyll air that seems to produce remarkable seamen. Duncan Newlands of Campbeltown lifeboat fame is not alone for his exploits saving lives in daring rescues that will never be forgotten. One of his successors as an RNLI coxswain was Tommy Ralston, who spent thirty-four years in various roles on the Mallaig lifeboat. Tommy now lives in Fife, but his memories of the west coast are fresh and vivid – something well demonstrated in the several books he has written in a new career as an author after retirement. Anyone who has talked to him knows he is a man of strong opinions and is not shy in letting them be known. Despite a lifetime of service in lifeboats (he was awarded a bronze medal by the RNLI in 1989), he has had some issues, as they say, with the organisation. He left school at fifteen and went into fishing right away on his father's 50-foot ring-netter *Golden Fleece*, out of Campbeltown. At that time many of the doughty fishers of the Wee Toon were not much in awe of lifeboats and lifeboatmen, especially as some of the RNLI crew were 'fermers', as they put it disparagingly. But the man who was to become a lifeboat legend himself remembers an incident at the beginning of his life at sea that changed his mind.

As a young teenager and crewman he was out on the *Golden Fleece* chasing a shoal of mackerel off Davaar Island, at the mouth of Campbeltown Loch, when in the darkness they struck a rock. Up to that point, his only real experience of the service was when down in Whitby, where the annual autumn herring bonanza attracted hundreds of Scottish boats and he was able to watch the last working rowing lifeboat in Britain on exercise in the harbour.

The *Golden Fleece* had been going pretty fast at the time and was well stuck on the rock. Ring-net fishing is now a little-used technique that requires two boats that work in partnership – experienced ring-net men were perhaps the most skilled of all who toiled in wild waters to put a herring or two on the table of city fat cats who had never sniffed the sea air on a dark and stormy night. The tide was falling fast and all the efforts of the *Golden Fleece*'s partner boat could not move the grounded vessel.

It was time. Out went a radio call for help from the lifeboat. Soon, the lights of the *City of Glasgow* were seen as she ploughed out of Campbeltown Loch to the rescue. The more powerful engines of the lifeboat did the trick and pulled the *Golden Fleece* off the rock. It was a lesson Tommy never forgot. In his book *To the Edge*, he observes: 'Not only was the towing operation a success, but contrary to what I had been led to believe, there was no claim for salvage. Indeed we were treated with what I later discovered was the usual hospitality and discreet courtesy of men who were doing a job they believed in totally.' Fortunately the rest of his Campbeltown career was free of Mayday calls to the RNLI.

After a few years, Tommy moved north to work with the Mallaig fleet, met and married a local girl, and in 1964 moved ashore to form a company buying, selling and processing fish and prawns. In Mallaig he spent more than three decades on the lifeboats, becoming coxswain/mechanic of the Arun-class lifeboat stationed there. Tommy loved the Arun and describes it as the 'best boat in the world'. He is very complimentary about its designer, a Mr MacLachlan of G.L. Watson who Tommy believes has never been given the credit he deserves for his work. The RNLI tweaked the design, altering the specifications of the underwater hull, which was not an improvement in Tommy's eyes. In Mallaig one day, Mr MacLachlan, a most self-effacing man, dropped in on the lifeboat station and Tommy took him on a little sea trip out to Loch Nevis, inviting the visitor to climb up to the flying bridge and put the boat through its paces. 'This is the first time I have driven the Arun,' he told Tommy.

Tommy, though, was to spend many a long, dangerous hour in the wheelhouse of an Arun. But one of the most remarkable rescues by a Mallaig boat occurred in January 1951 and involved an older design, the 48-foot Watson-class *Sir Arthur Rose*. This vessel had been on station for ten years at Tobermory before transferring to Mallaig because of trouble raising a crew on Mull. A large motor ship, the *Tapti*, had grounded in a gale on Eileen Soa, a small island at the mouth of the channel between Coll and Tiree. A navy ship and two trawlers were standing by, unable to help in the wild weather. It took the *Sir Arthur Rose* six hours to get to the scene from Mallaig. This veteran lifeboat had virtually no shelter for coxswain or crew and was barely more than an open boat. Surfing downwind in huge seas must have been a scary exercise for all on board.

81

The grounded ship had fifty-two lascar seamen aboard and ten officers and was listing 60 degrees, and it was bitterly cold with sleet showers. As dawn broke, coxswain Bruce Watt took decisive action and steered the lifeboat into broken water under the ship's bow. With no echo sounders in these days to help avoid the rocks close to the vessel, with great skill the *Sir Arthur Rose* was taken close enough for the entire crew to climb down a rope ladder and jump the final seven feet into the lifeboat. As this was going on, Bruce Watt used the engines to keep the lifeboat in position. It was magnificent seamanship. After twelve hours, crew and rescued finally returned to Mallaig and within twenty-four hours the *Tapti* slipped off the rocks. It had been a close-run thing.

Bruce Watt never got the medal he should have for that amazing rescue (though the RNLI thanked him in vellum) largely you suspect because of the natural self-effacing modesty you find in many a west coast man. This modesty was such that Tommy Ralston says: 'I believe that in his report he probably described the weather that night as being "no too bad"!'

The legend that is Tommy Ralston exhibits the same tendency to underplay the dangers of the lifeboats in his many tales of his own service. There is little in the way of 'waves as high as tenements' or 'tides rushing past like express trains' when he tells of his own exploits, and it is an admirable trait. But there is plenty of humour in his reminiscences. Some of the old lifeboats had temperamental stoves for cooking instead of relying on self-heating cans of soup and suchlike. Tommy remembers that if the crew did get the stove going, without the air being filled with stinking black smoke, a pot would be filled with soup, peas, chopped-up corned beef and any other bit of veg available. This mix was stirred until it was bubbling away merrily and at this point dollops of dehydrated potatoes were added. One crew member always insisted his tin soup plate was filled before the ersatz potatoes went into the mix, as he moaned that they tasted dreadful and gave him heartburn.

This would-be 'gourmet foodie' was heading for his comeuppance. One day the lifeboat had interrupted a sea search when darkness fell, and it went into Eigg harbour to await daybreak and another strenuous, dangerous day out searching for a casualty in the Atlantic. They were delighted when a local came down to the pier and asked them up to his home for a hot meal. This was a lovely stew full of beef and vegetables. On the groaning table was a steaming bowl of mashed and buttered potatoes. The food critic helped himself to the stew and then piled into the mashed potatoes. He enjoyed this so much he had an extra helping of the tatties, remarking along the lines of 'you canna beat the home-grown island potatoes. I think it must be the seaweed they use for manure. I wish we could get them in Mallaig.' At this his hostess interjected to point out that the delicacy was not local. The island tatties had run out and steamer had not called with stores because of bad weather. The praised dish had been made from powder!

After he had retired, Tommy Ralston settled on the east coast and is now an honorary Fifer. The sea still featured in his life and as Secretary of the Methil Sea Cadet Unit he raised £160,000 for the Sea Cadets. But visits back to Kintyre with a camera were regarded as battery-charging events and when there he did valuable work on the history of life-boats in the area. He told many of his tales in print or on the Internet. An intriguing story concerned the Machrihanish

lifeboat. These days this little village and its long and beautiful Atlantic beach is most noted for two of the best golf
courses in Scotland: the original links, which has a claim to
fame in that playing the dog-leg first you can take a short
cut to the fairway by driving across an inlet of the sea and
thereby claiming you have driven the Atlantic, and the new
internationally owned Machrihanish Dunes. But the village
has another claim to fame: this was the home of the 'Virgin
Lifeboat'.

After the loss of a trawler in a blizzard in 1908, driven
ashore on Westport beach, which is now overlooked by the
golf courses, it was decided to build a lifeboat station. The
station only existed for eighteen years and had only one lifeboat. This was the *Henry Finlay*, a 35-foot rowing/sailing
craft. It was to be manned by men from Campbeltown, four
or five miles away. Strangely, it was never launched on a
rescue mission and was eventually to end up in Tynemouth,
a journey it made by rail. Now that both Machrihanish and
Southend stations were no more it was said that not one lifeboat was on call on what one writer on nautical matters
called 'the weary stretch of the Scottish western seaboard
between Campbeltown and Stornoway'. Tommy Ralston
points out that this is an area now served, if you count
Lochinver, by seven powerful modern boats.

Still on the modern scene, Tommy has another observation. He remembers when in Mallaig he could have taken
the lifeboat from its moorings over to the pier and recruited
a top-class crew from the fishermen standing about. These
were skilled seamen used to the dangers of the sea every
day in life. Their like are not about in great numbers these
days, and lifeboats are crewed by folk with day jobs in a
bank, or a hospital, or maybe a garage. These are valuable

volunteers and their efforts undoubtedly save hundreds of lives each year, but they have to have costly training before they can go on rescue missions.

The skills of the old fishermen are dearly missed these days: they were men expert at small-boat handling in all weathers, an irreplaceable skill that you don't get at nautical college. Tommy told me with a laugh of once having the skipper of a very large container ship on board with him. This man could take a ship of around 100,000 tons round the world, but he was of no use in a wee fishing boat!

Tommy has kindly let me quote from his writings on a ring-net fisherman's life. It is a fascinating view of what it was like to wring a living out of Scotland's cruel sea – a way of life well worth recording:

When I began to serve my time as a fisherman in 1951, there were in excess of 200 Campbeltown fishermen earning their livings by catching herring. If one acknowledges that five jobs ashore are required to support one at sea – the least of the estimates that I have researched – then it follows that 1,200 jobs in the United Kingdom depended on the herring fishing efforts of the Campbeltown fleet alone.

Today, herring fishing as we knew it no longer exists. In the entire United Kingdom, I do not know of one job that depends solely on herring fishing. Were they fished out by the greed of men? I do not know the answer to that. Perhaps if fishermen had been allowed to continue governing their industry by themselves, as they had done for centuries, we would still have a viable herring fishery. Perhaps if fishermen had continued to live by the laws of nature instead of becoming 'carpet slippered screen-watchers and shelter deck labourers', nature would have allowed the herring fisheries to survive. After I wrote these words I learned that Lawrence Robertson, the very last of the Campbeltown ring-net herring fishermen, was still pursuing his calling as skipper of the Mary Ann. *He has now retired. This was the final break in a chain that stretched back, unbroken despite wars, for many centuries. Lawrence – I hope you put the lights out when you stepped ashore.*

What is it that makes many ring-net herring fishermen yearn, almost obsessively, for the days gone by? I am certain that, as I write this, John 'Shore' McConnochie of Carradale is sitting on Carradale Point, just a quarter of a mile from his home. His eyes will be searching up and down 'The Soon' – the name that he, and many others use for Kilbrannan Sound – searching for gannets, gulls or 'Sholters' (basking sharks) – all signs of shoals of herring.

The late Willie 'The Count' Jackson, of Target, when I questioned him not long before his death told me that on most days he would sit for hours in his car looking out over Lower Loch Fyne, searching for the same signs of herring and reliving exploits from the distant past. Jim Campbell recently built a house a few miles south of Carradale and pointed out to me that the back of this house overlooked a bay where he, many years ago, took around 1,200 baskets of herring in one ring. When I asked him how often he looked at the view and thought of this event he looked me in the eye and replied, after a pause: 'Aye, every bloody night o' ma life, jeest afore I go to ma bed!'

I am certain that, by now, readers will possibly be thinking that there is nothing unusual in reliving pleasant episodes from the past, but I would ask them to please consider the following facts before reaching their final conclusions. The ring-net boats, craft that have been generally acknowledged to be probably the most beautiful working boats ever built, ranged in size between 48 and 58 feet long with a beam of 15 to 18 feet. They were powered by engines that, in the early 1950s, were mainly of the ubiquitous 66 or 88 horsepower Kelvins or the 68 to 95 horsepower Gardners. In the 1970s, however, engines in excess of 250 h.p. were not uncommon. A dear friend, the late, and greatly missed, Donald Gibson, of Dunure, used to chuckle as he quoted his father as saying that the main things a ring-net boat required were: 'A 66 Kelvin in the engine room, a Bandeera stove in the fo'c's'le an' a brass rail roon the wheelus!' I will confine my thoughts to the boat that I served my time in, the Golden Fleece. She was 49 feet overall and had a 4 cylinder, 68 h.p. Gardner engine. In common with all of the ringers of that era the engine room was aft and the fo'c's'le forward – the space between them was the hold which held around 420 baskets (105 crans) of bulk herring.

The tiny fo'c's'le was where five men and a boy lived, ate and slept for periods of up to six weeks at a time. It was about 15 feet in length and its width tapered from around 12 feet at the aft end to a point at the fore end. There were six bunks, three on each side with lockers for storing food etc. below the two forward bunks. There were additional lockers, two of which were used for storing coal, below the wooden seating that ran around the sides below the bunks. A rudimentary table with side flaps stood in the middle of the floor space. The bunks, especially on an old boat like the Golden Fleece, were invariably damp – if not wet – and certainly when I started fishing the mattresses were usually of flock that was lumpy beyond belief! A small, one ring coal stove was situated along the bulkhead that divided the fo'c's'le from the hold. All of the cooking was done on this stove but we carried a simple paraffin-powered Primus stove that was mainly used to boil the kettle for a quick cup of tea.

We ate well, I really must say, but my wife was disgusted to hear that if at the weekend we had, for example, mutton broth (a favourite of mine) we ate the soup from a soup bowl, which was then used for the meat, tatties and vegetables. The sweet, typically tinned custard or rice with tinned fruit was eaten from the same plate. Well, they all mixed up in your stomach, anyway! Mind you, the plates usually got a dicht with a slice of bread between courses! There were no personal washing facilities apart from an enamel basin that had to be a different colour from the similar one that was used for washing up dishes! Anyway, in the Minches there were very few places where the fresh water tank could be easily replenished so personal cleanliness took a back seat!

I recall telling the late George Alexander (Doddie Icey), another very dear friend of mine, a man who was orphaned when he was just eighteen years old and who skippered his own steam drifter when he was twenty-one, that we would be unable to have a bath for between four and six weeks when fishing in the Minches. How, I asked, did he fare when he worked the Yarmouth fishery, which meant that he would be away from home for around three months? 'Ah weel,' he replied, after some thought, 'We wis aye affa fussy aboot that. We aye hid a bath jeest afore we left hame, an we aye made sure we hid anither een as soon's we got back!'

The toilet was fashioned from a round 5 gallon oil drum that had its top chiselled off and had a piece of rubber hose or a length of old bicycle tyre, the preferred choices, attached to the part you sat on. Toilet paper was a page from the Daily Record or, if you were on a really posh boat (which I wasn't), the Daily Express! There were no fixed working hours then. It was quite usual to spend the night fishing and then to set off to market getting – if the weather allowed – your three hours sleep when off watch en route. The herring then had to be discharged before *getting another three hours sleep en route back to the fishing grounds and another night's toil. If there was a breeze of south-westerly wind, sleep – even with a wooden fish room board fixed in an attempt to avoid being thrown from your bunk – was difficult indeed! If you caught no herring you got no money and home life was curtailed to a point where it would not be tolerated now. Not for the first time, I question why we put up with this environment when today there would be a public outcry if the vilest of prisoners were subjected to similar conditions? I have never found an answer to that question. Health and safety? You are joking!*

*We were certainly – I see with hindsight – much closer to nature and we generally worked within nature's rules. Every sense we possessed was used to detect our prey, with the exception of taste. It was exciting; I cannot imagine anything more exciting and fulfilling than drying up a good ring of herring. Most importantly perhaps, there was a real camaraderie among fishermen then. E.E.C. rulings have now taken the place of the laws of nature and they are the cause of almost intolerable stress. I remember asking the aforementioned Willie Jackson why he didn't continue fishing after a decline in earnings meant that the boats had to abandon the ring-net and resort to prawn trawling at times in order to try to make ends meet. He replied: 'Trawlin' for prawns? That's no' fishin' – that's sheer f****n' boredom.'*

I now find myself back where I started! Why is it that, despite the facts that the conditions we worked in and the lives we led were intolerable by today's standards, just about any one of the rapidly diminishing band of men who took part in the glory days of the ring-net fishery will tell you that, given the chance, they would do it all over again? You will have to tell me why this is, because I simply do not know.

The exploits of Duncan Newlands, Bruce Watt, Tommy Ralston and their brave and skilled crews brought the attention of newspaper readers to Campbeltown, Mallaig and Oban lifeboat bases in particular. An interesting footnote is Oban's connection with one of the great mysteries of the Second World War. Elsewhere in this book I tell of the sinking of HMS *Hampshire* off Orkney and the death of Lord Kitchener, an event still surrounded by conspiracy theories. In the early thirties the RAF scoured the Scottish coast for places suitable for the then popular flying boats, such as the Supermarine Stranraer, Saro Lerwick and latterly the Sunderland. Kerrera island, just off Oban, was judged suitable for refuelling and servicing and a slip and jetty were constructed. The base became operational in 1938 and by 1940 was home to 210 Squadron's Sunderlands. When it was operational some of the many fine hotels facing onto Oban bay became billets for the servicemen. I wonder if any of the holiday-makers who now frequent these busy and popular places ever give a thought to their wartime history, or indeed to the exploits of the local lifeboat. Cromarty Firth was also deemed suitable as a base for these large and majestic-looking aircraft, though they were slow and cumbersome, albeit providing comfortable long-distance travel on patrol.

Kitchener died on a 'secret' mission, as did the most important passenger a Sunderland carried – the Duke of Kent. He was the younger brother of the reigning king, George VI. He left the Cromarty Firth base in a Sunderland (Flight W-4206) on 25 August 1942. Popular, he and his wife Princess Marina had a few weeks previously celebrated the birth of a son. Adjectives like gallant and handsome were thrown about when this man, who was an air commodore, was discussed in newspapers and drawing rooms. But that was very much an outsider's perception. This royal may not have been as squeaky clean as was thought at the time. There were, in high society, allegations of drug use and sexual impropriety.

The destination of this secret mission was Iceland. Wild rumours abounded: in one, that Rudolph Hess, Hitler's deputy, was on board the Sunderland. This theory seemed to make little sense, despite some claims that the man who died in Spandau Prison in Berlin in his nineties was an imposter. The Hess family did not seem to swallow that one. The truth of what happened on Flight W-4206 to cause it to end in a fireball on a remote Highland hillside will never be known – sabotage, pilot error, a Nazi plot, drinking? A final touch to this intriguing mystery is that one survivor was allegedly silenced by the RAF and died many years later, having added nothing to help solve the riddle.

All that was many years ago, but Oban lifeboat made headlines other than those recording its life-saving adventures in early 2014. One of the busiest stations in the country, it had had an all-male crew since it opened in 1972. This seems a bit surprising since Campbeltown, Tobermory and Islay all had women among their volunteer crews long ago, and Tighabruaich had an inshore boat with an all-woman crew. The Oban history maker was Lucy Hyam, who already had some experience with the Cromer lifeboat station south of the border and who came north to study marine science. Coxswain John Hill said: 'She is already a valuable and dedicated member of the team.' The Oban station, with its proximity to the isles, is heavily used for medical evacuation duties. The current boat has had four babies born on it. This prompted an amusing memory from Tommy Ralston on the subject of women crew on lifeboats. He took to cyberspace to recount that when he was cox/mechanic with Mallaig lifeboat he was part of a conversation at a meeting of lifeboat folk about possible problems with babies being born on such 'medvac' trips. Tommy heard a sotto voce comment from the Tobermory cox, who had two female crew members, that the problem might be preventing conception rather than birth!

Lucy Hyam is only one of thousands who make up the lifeboat service. And just as important as the crews themselves are the folk who do the fundraising to provide the state-of-the-art boats on standby round our coasts. In towns, cities and remote fishing villages there are thousands of dedicated folk who shake cans and run Harbour Days, dinners, dances, ceilidhs and concerts to keep the boats ready for an emergency call. One of those was a remarkable Oban lady called Marie-Claire Williamson-MacDougall, who died in the summer of 2014. Marie-Claire had worked tirelessly for decades to raise money for their local boat, raising thousands of pounds. Nearing the end of her life in June, she still collected money for the teas and coffees at the station's open day. The folk of Oban remember her going round local shops selling home-made marmalade for the RNLI. So much was she respected that the lifeboat crew were to be her pall-bearers. But fate intervened in the form of an emergency call on the day of her funeral. Stornoway coastguard said that a call for help at 5.34 a.m. was answered and two sailors were rescued from a yacht off Jura. The funeral went ahead with the family standing in for the lifeboat crew as pall-bearers. But the mourners came out from the service to a poignant scene – the lifeboat had returned just in time to lie off Oban cathedral. There were tears on many faces. It was a scene that would have delighted Marie-Claire, and a scene that somehow captured the essence of the service thousands of supporters give to the lifeboats onshore and at sea.

On the east coast, too, you get similar dedication to funding the lifeboat service. And sadly there is tragedy there that will likewise never be forgotten. In an incident hauntingly similar to the loss of a lifeboat off Orkney called *TGB* – after the initials of an anonymous donor – in which an entire crew on a rescue mission out of Longhope were killed, another entire crew was lost when in December 1959 the boat stationed at Broughty Ferry went to aid the crew of a lightship drifting off St Andrews. The entire area was swept with gales and the *Mona* was the only boat able to be launched. She searched for the endangered lightship in horrendous conditions, and in the dark shortly before dawn radio contact was lost. A helicopter search found the *Mona* capsized on Buddon Sands. The crew of eight had drowned. An official investigation found that the *Mona* had been completely seaworthy when she sailed on her last rescue mission. She had simply been overwhelmed in huge seas. In another of the great ironies of life on Scotland's cruel sea, the six men on the lightship managed to drop a spare anchor and end the drift. They were rescued by helicopter.

There is a strange footnote to this sad story, as the vessel was taken later to Cockenzie harbour on the Firth of Forth, chained to the sea wall and set ablaze. In 2006 a letter in a local paper explained this, saying, 'Among some seamen it was believed the *Mona* was tainted with evil and they resolved to exorcise the boat in a Viking ritual.' This was done with the approval of the lifeboat authorities. This remarkable incident and the bravery of the *Mona*'s crew is commemorated in a song performed by the Dubliners and written by Peggy Seeger. With such strong feelings in local communities it is little wonder that the RNLI is so well supported financially by folk grateful for the work they do.

Another example is the recent story of the 'biscuit boys'. A grandfather and his grandson were lost at sea for three days, feared drowned. They existed on a bottle of water and a couple of bars of that famed Scottish delicacy, the caramel wafer, while a massive sea and air search went on for them. They had set out from Gourdon in Aberdeenshire in a small creel boat but lost their way in fog. Family and friends spent sixty hours praying for their safety, and just as hope was fading they were found by a trawler fifty miles out in the North Sea, far from the search area.

Some weeks after this remarkable happening, volunteers in the coastal villages of Inverbervie, Gourdon and Johnshaven, delighted at the happy ending to what could have been another tragedy, ran a barn dance to commemorate the escape of the 'biscuit boys'. It raised almost £6,500 for lifeboat stations at Stonehaven and Montrose. Henry Weaver of the RNLI told the *Daily Record*: 'We are extremely grateful to the community. The money will go a long way to help provide our volunteers with the training and equipment they require to keep them safe saving the lives of others. It costs the RNLI just under £1,400 to kit out one of our volunteers and we spend just over £1,400 a year training each crew member.'

That's a long way from the days when skilled crews could be plucked at random from the fishing communities. Changed days in many ways, but anyone who goes to sea – and their relatives – gives thanks for lifeboat crews who risk their lives to go to the rescue of others.

Princess Victoria. Clyde-built pioneer car ferry, victim of a
horrendous winter gale in the Irish Sea.

Byron Darnton. The most
famous wreck on the infamous
Boiler Reef, on Sanda off the
Mull of Kintyre.

A remarkable illustration of the SS *Daphne* disaster
on the Clyde in 1883.

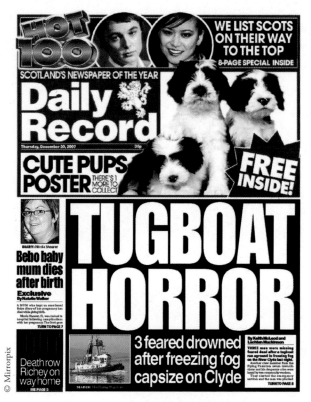

Coverage of the *Flying Phantom* disaster.

A tranquil Tail of the Bank and the memorial to the
Free French Forces in World War II.

Salvage workers on the wrecked deck of the French warship *Maillé Brézé*, the destroyer that torpedoed itself in 1940 off Greenock.

SACRED

TO THE MEMORY OF

THOSE NAMED

WHO LOST THEIR LIVES

IN H.M. SUBMARINE, K,13.

IN THE GARELOCH

29TH JANUARY 1917

The memorial in Govan to the men who died on submarine *K13* in 1917.

HMS *Hampshire*. Her sinking spawned startling conspiracy theories.

How the *Daily Record* reported the *Iolaire* tragedy.

Daily Rec
and Mail.
The All-Scotland Newspaper. Sale Twice That of Any Other Mo

ESTAB. 1847—No. 22,454   GLASGOW, THURSDAY, JANUARY 2, 1919.

TERRIBLE NEW-YEAR'S DAY DISASTER

DISASTER AT STORNOWAY.

LEAVE SHIP WITH LEWIS MEN RUNS ASHORE.

FEARED LOSS OF 300 LIVES.

A telegram from Stornoway, Isle of Lewis, reports that H.M. steam yacht Amalthea (the re-named Iolaire), the parent ship of the Stornoway Naval Base, went aground while entering the harbour there early yesterday morning.

The vessel was on the passage from the Kyle of Lochalsh, and had on board Naval ratings, all Lewis men going home on New Year leave.

It is feared there has been loss of 300 lives, but according to official information received in London late yesterday afternoon, the chances appear to be that there have been fewer casualties. Several members of the crew succeeded in swimming ashore.

THE PREMIER IN WALES.

REAFFIRMATION OF HIS PLEDGES.

PEOPLE'S MAN ALL THE TIME.

Mr. Lloyd George, accompanied by Mrs. Lloyd George, passed through Carnarvon yesterday on his way to Criccieth.

Outside the Liberal Club, which he had to pass on entering the town, an enthusiastic crowd awaited the Premier's arrival, and gave him a rousing reception.

Addressing the crowd from the balcony of the Club, the Prime Minister said that in passing through he was pleased to have the opportunity of thanking his old friends for their kindness and loyalty.

He had represented the Carnarvon

BULGAR

WHOLESAL SER

Reuter's Agen graphic reports quarters of the International Con furnish fresh evic reign of terror in from the atroci Bulgarians.

Requisitions, blooded murder a description bare b doubt. Secret now brought to lig cases even the against the behav countrymen.

The Bulgarian openly accused Bu murder of Serbs, Gorge of Sardini grave of the Serbi Bulgarian official of the murder, B garian officer, of a

Part of a telegram from the Eyemouth Fishery Office with news of the 1881 disaster. 'Exceedingly sorry to say that about 60 Eyemouth, 3 Coldingham and some Burnmouth fishermen lost in yesterday's fearful hurricane. Upwards of 20 Boats still missing. Will write further particulars today.'

Lord Kitchener. His death at sea shocked a nation at war.

Newspaper coverage of Kitchener after his death at sea.

The Longhope lifeboat *TGB*, now in the Scottish Maritime Museum at Irvine, lost an entire crew on a rescue mission, overturned in gigantic seas, searching for the freighter *Irene* (above) which ended up on rocks and the crew saved.

Fire, darkness and death in the North Sea after the Piper Alpha blow out.

The legendary oil rig firefighter, Red Adair, in action.

Coverage of the Super Puma North Sea crash.

7

IOLAIRE: TRAGEDY AT NEW YEAR

One of the most enjoyable journeys at sea off the west coast is the car ferry trip from Ullapool to Lewis. The ship, these days normally the sturdy *Isle of Lewis*, is much used by the locals and in the summer is packed with cars and tourists excited about a holiday roaming the outer isles, visiting the pristine beaches, enjoying the spectacular views out to the Atlantic or back across the Minch to the majestic mountains of the mainland. Or maybe visiting such world-famous historical sites as the mysterious and awesome standing stones of Callanish or the Iron Age dun at Carloway broch.

Sadly, most visitors give little thought to a monument that can be seen on the starboard side of their ship on the approach to the town's pier. This commemorates one of the most tragic maritime disasters of the twentieth century, the sinking of the naval yacht *Iolaire* on New Year's Day 1919. As in many tragedies the exact death toll is difficult to establish, but these days it is accepted that at least 205 of the 280 or so aboard died. It is a poignant tale, and the text on the memorial could bring many a tear, as well as some indication of the desperately sad effect on the island and its people then and now:

Erected by the people of Lewis and friends in grateful memory of the men of the Royal Navy who lost their lives in the 'Iolaire' disaster at the Beasts of Holm on 1 January 1919. Of the 205 persons lost, 175 were natives of the island and for them and their comrades Lewis still mourns. With gratitude for their service and in sorrow for their loss.

Perhaps the timing of the accident, so soon after the end of the First World War, a war in which millions had died and from which the whole of Europe was just beginning to recover, is part of the cause of the tragedy having drifted so far from public memory across most of Britain, though it still looms large in the collective memory of the Western Isles. It should also be recognised that the drama that played out on that bitter January day came at a time when modern communication methods were just evolving. No live TV footage. No clips from smartphones. No live interviews with survivors or grieving relatives of the victims. No high-quality colour photographs splashed on front pages of tabloids and broadsheets. However, the story of the *Iolaire* was what modern media would call 'of truly immense human interest'.

Hundreds of Lewis men were returning on a national holiday from the war to their Hebridean island, full of hope and happiness, only to die in icy-cold, wind-lashed waters within hundreds of yards of hearth and home. The winter lights of Stornoway were reflected on stormy waters as islanders died in droves. The coverage of the accident was very different from that of more modern tragedies. Indeed, it was a humble telegram, a method of communication itself largely forgotten, that first told the news of the poignant disaster. And the early reports, for the most part, were very matter of fact, not 'human interest' orientated, as they would be nowadays. However, as we shall see, Scotland's two quality broadsheets did record the dreadful effect on the islanders in sympathetic and emotional reports.

The *Iolaire* was originally a steam yacht called *Amalthea* but was subsequently renamed by the navy using the Gaelic name for eagle. It had also at times been known as *Iolanthe* and *Mione*. Some seafarers are suspicious about changing a ship's name and certainly it was unlucky for the *Iolaire*. Now HMS *Iolaire* was on Admiralty service as the parent ship of Stornoway naval base when it ran aground on jagged rocks known as the Beasts of Holm: rocks that were, significantly, well known and right on the doorstep of its home port. These rocks, though dangerous, were marked and, the *Iolaire* incident apart, had claimed few lives. The yacht was stylish and of around 900 tons and had been built for Sir Donald Currie. Not long after the start of the Great War, it was handed over to the Admiralty in a generous act of patriotism for 'national purposes'. Currie, a Scot, was a fascinating character who had started in shipping with Cunard before moving into ship-owning himself. Apart from a lifetime involvement with the sea and ships, he was a major patron of both rugby and football, being involved in, among other sporting ploys, the football team that eventually became London's West Ham United.

News may have travelled much more slowly in these days, but reports could still capture some of the horror. The ship sank on 1 January 1919 and the *Glasgow Herald* of 4 January reported from the scene:

An old man sobbing into his handkerchief with a stalwart son in khaki sitting on the cart beside him, the remains of another son in the coffin behind – that was one of the sights seen today as one of the funeral parties emerged from the barrack gate. Another, an elderly woman well-dressed, comes staggering down the roadway and bursts into a paralysis of grief as she tells sympathisers that her boy is in the mortuary. Strong men weeping and women wailing or wandering around with blanched, tear-stained faces are to be seen in almost every street and there are groups of them at the improvised mortuary.

Almost 100 years ago, *The Scotsman* also piled on the emotion in its reporting of the disaster:

The villages of Lewis are like places of the dead. The homes of the island are full of lamentation – grief that cannot be comforted. Scarce a family has escaped the loss of a dear blood relative. Many have had sorrow heaped on sorrow.

How did it come to this? How were the high hopes of island men returning from service for their country in the Great War to end on the rocky shore of their home island, washed onto beaches, dashed onto rocks within sight of safety? Survivors of the horrors of war in foreign lands died on the blackest New Year's Day in Scotland's history. But the reason has never been fully explained.

To put the scale of the disaster in proportion, it can be remarked that the sinking of the *Iolaire* was the worst maritime disaster in British waters since the sinking of the SS *Norge* near Rockall in 1904 and the worst involving a British ship since the *Titanic* in 1912. It has often been wrongly reported that the loss of life when the *Herald of Free Enterprise* sank in 1987 was the worst since the *Titanic*. In that tragedy, 193 souls lost their lives in the glare of worldwide publicity, but even that terrible disaster had fewer deaths than those suffered when the *Iolaire* went down.

And other maritime tragedies paint a terrible picture of loss of life through the years. The sinking of HMS *Hampshire*, to be dealt with in the next chapter, is in fact the worst in terms of loss of life. Then there was the *Norge*, a Clyde-built passenger liner (by Stephens of Linthouse) bound for New York, which, like the *Iolaire*, had had a name change. It was originally called *Pieter de Coninck* by its Danish owners. More than 600 died when it hit a reef near Rockall and 160 survivors spent more than a week in open lifeboats. Others died in them.

But thoughts of a place in the history of the maritime disasters were the last thing on the minds of the soldiers who piled up the gangways of the *Iolaire* as it was moored at the pier of Kyle of Lochalsh, the beautiful gateway to the far isles, now almost in the shadow of the Skye Bridge. Perhaps as a portent of trouble to come, the *Iolaire* hit the Kyle pier a hard 'dunt', as the Highlanders would say, on arrival. The military personnel had travelled north by train from establishments in the south in high spirits and in boisterous mood, with laughter and chatter in the air. The wartime years of danger and deprivation and separation from loved ones were almost over. The journey across the Minch was the last short step in an emotional trek home.

Maybe those very high spirits played a role in the accident. The whole town was in a holiday mood. Unlike today, back in these times the New Year holiday in Scotland was far more important than Christmas. And this was a New Year of great significance – the slaughter of the war in

Europe had finally ended. Hope and thanksgiving were in the air, nowhere more so than in this Highland seaport. The mainlanders knew the Lewis men well. They were aware that nearly 1,000 from the island had lost their lives out of the 6,200 who had joined up to fight the German menace. But at last it was all over. Peace had arrived and it was time to return to a more normal way of life as soon as possible. Maybe this dream diluted the natural common sense of both the returning servicemen and the crew of the *Iolaire*. Who knows? But it is fact that the naval vessel was desperately overcrowded when it sailed.

Demobbed troops were still on trains heading north, as, in this atmosphere of euphoria, the naval authorities were discussing the forthcoming voyage of the *Iolaire*. The skipper, Commander Mason, was voicing concern to the navy commander in Kyle about safety. The vessel had only two lifeboats, hopeless in terms of the numbers she was to carry. In addition there were only eighty life jackets on board the vessel, which should have only taken around 100 people, though in the event there was more than double that number aboard when the lines were cast ashore and she headed out for Lewis, leaving those back in Kyle to enjoy a New Year dram or three. Anyone at Hogmanay ceilidhs would not be dreaming for a moment of the danger their Hebridean friends were sailing into.

There was one other worrying and surprising factor: HMS *Iolaire* had never before sailed into Stornoway, a notoriously difficult harbour in the days before GPS, in the dark. As the preparations to sail got underway, two more trains arrived, spilling hundreds onto the quayside. How could you refuse these men the trip home they had dreamed of, how could you deny them boarding and where would they stay? It had all the makings of a shambles. It was bad planning by the military top brass.

The authorities caved in to the pressure the new arrivals brought. In the event, 248 servicemen pushed up the gangway. No one was to know what was to go wrong in Stornoway harbour and the overcrowding would have little effect on the navigation of the vessel. But it undoubtedly meant that the death toll was higher than it would have been if the yacht had had its normal contingent aboard when it sailed in the dark into the jaws of the Beasts of Holm.

It left Kyle around 9.30 p.m. in reasonable weather, but that was soon to change. Twelve miles away from the safety of Stornoway harbour, wind and sea got up, not at all unusual or unexpected in the Minch at that time of year. About this point the crew of a local fishing boat spotted the lights of the *Iolaire* as she headed to her base at full steam. But the fishermen, who knew the area intimately, were surprised that the naval yacht did not seem to be making an appropriate change of course for Stornoway pier – it was supposed to anchor in the harbour and the passengers were to be ferried ashore – but instead continued on a course that was wrong for the intended destination.

Though the Beasts of Holm had developed over the years a fearsome reputation, the rocks were not marked with a powerful light, as you might expect. Instead there was a low-power flashing light that was no help to a vessel on the wrong course for the harbour: exactly the situation the *Iolaire* was in. And with sleet and drizzle in the air, visibility was poor. It was a typically foul Hebridean winter night, with winds by now nearing gale force and the sea heavy. The elements seemed to combine with a mistake in navigation by the crew to drive the yacht onto the rocks. But many have testified that the weather was not so bad as to be the cause of the sinking. From the day of the sinking until now, there has been no truly satisfactory explanation of why the approach to the pier was wrong, except for an accusation, which will be dealt with more fully later, that those in charge of the lives of the returning war heroes had been drinking.

There is no speculation about what happened when the yacht smashed into the rocks. After she had struck, she rolled over almost immediately. Some reports say that she was just yards from the shore, but the few feet of white water between the men and safety was whipped into a cauldron by wind and currents. To swim ashore would have tested an Olympic gold-medal winner or the most experienced life-saver. Many of those aboard, including the crew, could not swim in any case. Surprisingly, this was true for many fishermen who plied their trade in the isles. Life jackets were a rarity on coastal vessels in those days – and there were only eighty aboard, as has been pointed out earlier – as were swimming lessons, life-saving safety exercises and mandatory safety inspections.

There was another factor in this – there was a notion in Highland harbours that maybe the inability to swim was a good thing, as a swift death from drowning was better than prolonging the agony, swimming around in circles until exhaustion took its toll and the victim slipped under the waves to the same sort of death as those who could not swim.

There was nothing for it for the hapless passengers and crew but to jump into the wild spray and freezing waters. Almost immediately fifty or so did just that and quickly perished. The two lifeboats were launched but were swamped in minutes as desperate men fought for too few places. And at 3 a.m., the yacht's back broke and she slipped under the waves. One despairing man clung to the mast as she sank and managed to hang on as the mast stuck out from the depths. This man, Donald Morrison, was rescued alive after daylight and eight hours in the water. It was an almost incredible escape, but, poignantly, Mr Morrison's brother drowned.

There were other horrific stories. The Lewis Roll of Honour writes of the death of Kenneth Macphail, one of the hundreds who drowned. His is a heart-rending and moving tale of a war hero dying yards from home after adventures and narrow escapes in foreign parts. Kenneth Macphail had a dramatic war and at times must have wondered if he would ever see Lewis again. Two years earlier he was the sole survivor of a ship torpedoed in the Mediterranean. He was washed ashore in Algeria after a day and a half in the sea. As the Roll of Honour puts it: 'Pathetic in the extreme it is to think that this powerful seaman after so miraculous an escape in the Mediterranean perished within a few feet of his native soil.'

On a New Year's Day unlike any other in the history of the Western Isles, news of the disaster spread slowly across Lewis. From miles around, from the far west, the north and south, islanders trudged across crofting land heading for the island 'capital', their muscles aching and their minds heavy with foreboding. What they found was the hellish sight of some bodies still being recovered, others already on carts for transportation to the makeshift morgue. Others were already in the morgue. The anguish of the islanders as they searched for loved ones, praying that they had survived, must have been agonising to watch. For most of the folk from outlying areas, as well as the townspeople, it ended in tears.

In 1959, Donald Macphail recalled in a radio interview the moment when a friend found his son's body: 'The man's son was there and I remember he was so handsome that I could have said he was not dead at all. His father went on his knees beside him and began to take letters from his pockets. His tears were splashing on the body of his son. And I think it was the most heart-rending sight I have seen.'

Equally upsetting is the story still told in Lewis of a man from the hamlet of Breasclete. Six weeks after the disaster, he is said to have had visions of a body floating in the sea. He went to Stornoway. There he directed a boat to the area he had seen in his dream and a body was recovered from the very spot: the body of his son. The western islanders are a deeply religious people and also of a somewhat superstitious nature, so it is no surprise that folk talked of seeing deer – believed to be a portent of death – in unexpected places on the night of the sinking. Many other such tales with supernatural overtones are woven into the story of the *Iolaire*.

Amid the tears and tragedy there were also stories of great heroism, in particular the story of survivor John Macleod, who managed to swim through the wild waters to the shore, taking a light line with him. Arriving exhausted on the sand after his efforts in the freezing water, he used the light line to get a stronger rope on the remains of the yacht and twenty-five men managed to escape death using it.

Looking back at the story of the *Iolaire*, two important and perplexing questions arise: why did it happen and what long-term effect did it have on the island and the islanders? Quite frankly, I am of the opinion there is no definitive answer to either question almost 100 years after the event. The fact is that there were two 'inquiries', neither at all satisfactory. A naval inquiry shortly after the event was almost immediately downgraded to a court of inquiry, presumably because having a court martial might imply that the navy admitted guilt. This inquiry was held on 8 January 1919, though the results were not released until 1970. It had apparently ruled that due to the non-survival of any officers on board 'no opinion can be given as to whether blame is attributable to anyone in the matter'.

A public inquiry was held in Stornoway not much later, on 10 February 1919, and seven local men were chosen for a jury. This time the results were available to the public. The most significant was that drink was claimed not to be to blame, despite much public suspicion to the contrary. The jury categorically ruled out the demon drink as a cause.

It also discussed the fact that although the weather was not good, it was not as spectacularly bad as you can get in the area in winter. Also in the frame for blame was the suspicion that the vessel had been travelling too fast, no lookouts posted or at least not enough, and of course the lack of lifeboats and life jackets, which contributed to the numbers who failed to survive an accident so near the shore.

The inquiries were rushed and shallow and now look insensitive. They produced bland, unsatisfactory findings. No wonder the accusation of whitewash was thrown around for years. This was bad enough, but even more insensitive was what was to happen to the wreck. Mind you, although the navy had been found to blame, no names were highlighted or specific errors identified. The Admiralty put the wreck up for sale a mere fifteen days after the disaster and at a time when more than fifty bodies had not been recovered. These were certainly very different times.

On the drink question, it is easy to see how the theory that it was the prime cause took hold. In Scotland, Hogmanay can be a time when 'the cratur' slips over dusty throats in a golden Niagara that would destroy brain cells by the thousand. But it also has to be said that the navy has been around for hundreds of years and seems largely to have retained the ability to keep ships safe even at the height of New Year festivities. Why should it have been any different aboard the *Iolaire*? Indeed, there was some reasonable discussion on safety before she set sail. And it is unlikely that there was a cocktail bar running during the voyage, though there would certainly have been some rum, but not in great quantities. The passengers themselves were likely to have been sober, as they had just been decanted from troop trains more or less directly onto the converted yacht. It is also interesting that at the time there was a strong anti-drink movement among the god-fearing folk of the Hebrides, presumably including some on the jury, which ruled out drink as the prime cause.

For a more in-depth analysis than can be offered here, the remarkable book *When I Heard the Bell: The Loss of the Iolaire* by a one-time colleague of mine on the *Glasgow Herald*, controversial columnist and Hebridean historian John MacLeod, is to be recommended. In it he tells of being told as a child that drink was to blame. And he has made a study of the inquiries and the first-hand stories of families who lost sons and of the survivors' accounts. In his book he tracks a renewed interest in the *Iolaire* from the 1950s onwards. This resulted eventually in a *Stornoway Gazette* booklet called *Sea*

Sorrow, which contained many of the paper's reports from the time.

And all the while, myths about the sinking grew. There was even reported the bizarre claim that arguments between the skipper, Commander Mason, and locals on board led to the yacht being deliberately driven onto the rocks. But the documents from 1919 seem to confirm that Mason was amiable, not suicidal.

Perhaps slightly more believable was the story that locals aboard, realising the ship was steaming too fast towards the rocks, tried to storm the bridge to warn of the danger. But there is no solid evidence from the time that this happened.

Some of growing number of tales had some real truth – in particular the one that said that the few life jackets available were pretty useless. John MacLeod is particularly scathing about one myth, and myth it seems to have been, that someone saw Commander Mason's body with two life jackets on it. As the author points out, it is a hard one to swallow since Mason has no grave (and it is difficult to tell a navy officer's rank from his jacket) and the person telling the tale was a teenager who had never met the skipper.

MacLeod is strong on the legend that the demon drink was to blame but makes some other cogent points, in particular the fact that the early inquiry ruled out drink. As he points out, the jury contained at least one person known for his anti-drink views. This islander, as you would suspect, pounced on any evidence that the demon drink was to blame. On the other hand, John MacLeod makes much of the fact that our view of what 'under the influence' means was rather different in 1919 than now in the age of the breathalyser. Then, staggering and slurring words were the key signs.

For the case against Commander Mason, it has to be said

it was claimed he was not on the bridge when the vessel struck. And he seemed to have taken no part in the evacuation and rescue operation. When rockets were fired, he was not to be seen. But he did go to the wireless operator, a man called Welch, and try to get him to coax a damaged machine to life in order to send a distress signal. The operator was questioned at the inquiry and said the skipper seemed agitated. He was then asked directly if this was a consequence of what was happening to his ship or otherwise. Welch, possibly aware of an insinuation that, as they say in the Glasgow courts, 'drink was a factor', replied he thought it was because of what was happening. John MacLeod finds it suspicious that Welch was not called to a later inquiry, as he was the only man in a position to have smelled the breath of Mason. Was the agitation he referred to shock in the middle of a disaster or because of drink? We will probably never know for sure. Nor will we know the reason for the unusual and fatal approach to the harbour.

As ever in cases like this, there are theories galore. Some are what we would now call conspiracy theories; others include possible compass errors, lighthouses being mixed up and incompetent manoeuvres at sea. There was even the suggestion that the drizzle interfered with the light from the lighthouses, making the signals hard to understand and therefore impeding the identification of the warning beams.

There is no better examination of all this than in John MacLeod's remarkable book. It also deals with that second question of mine – the effect on the island. There is no doubt that the emotional effect still exists in the close-knit culture of Lewis today. Perhaps one reason for this is what is now called 'survivor guilt'.

I put the question to an academic psychologist in a

Scottish university and also asked, in a cynical, journalistic way, if he believed such a condition is 'real'. I was told:

The immediate answer is that it is a widely used and accepted psychological term that describes the experience of many people caught up in disasters, natural or otherwise. The term was not coined until 1968, when German-American psychoanalyst William Niederland identified 'survivor syndrome' working with holocaust survivors, so at the time of the sinking of the Iolaire *there would have been little understanding of the psychological impact of this kind of experience on survivors. Niederland noticed a very particular set of symptoms that often occurred together including: anxiety, disturbance of memory and cognition, depression, psychosomatic conditions and even detachment from reality. The symptoms of survivor guilt and post-traumatic stress disorder overlap, but some authors have hypothesised that the term 'survivor guilt' better explains the symptoms when the survivor was one of a particularly tightly knit group of people, most of whom have been killed, as in the Lewis sinking. They concluded that 'intra-group cohesiveness' increases the chances of survivor guilt over post-traumatic stress. The question 'why did I live when others died?' becomes more painful and problematic the closer and more attached we are to the deceased. Both survivor guilt and post-traumatic stress have been widely reported in survivors of the recent tsunamis in Japan and Indonesia, where the terms have been used to explain a rash of suicides amongst those who survived the initial tragedy but who lost the will to live faced with such arbitrary horror and cruelty.*

The concept of such survivor guilt must also play a role in other incidents described later in this book in detail. The loss of the Longhope lifeboat off the Orkneys is one example. There was hardly a person on the island who did not lose a relative or friend, so closely knit was that northern community. The same was the case, though the numbers were higher, in the Eyemouth fishing disaster of 1881. And a more up-to-date example would be the Piper Alpha fire. In the case of the oil rig, the relatives of those who died, and those who survived, had the additional pressure of live TV pictures of the burning rig, and radio and TV interviews, plus daily saturation coverage in the newspapers to endure. Clearly there is much helpful work to be done by psychologists in this area.

No matter how you analyse it, there is no doubt that the sinking of the *Iolaire* was one of the most traumatic events in the history of the Western Isles, and particularly in Lewis. John MacLeod, a doughty islander himself, declares in a powerful passage in his fine book that: 'Her outstanding part in the Great War has been mocked, tainted, defiled. In the most immediate and personal way dozens of homes are bereaved in the cruellest of fashion: dozens widowed, hundreds are orphaned, and the island is devastated.'

Even today, few Lewis men can yet utter the name of the *Iolaire* without emotion. Of that, there is no argument.

8

HMS *HAMPSHIRE* AND
THE DEATH OF KITCHENER

It is surprising how often in the history of major maritime disasters that sheer wrong-headedness or bloody-mindedness, call it what you will, played a role. Maybe it was, as in the *Princess Victoria*, that over-familiarity with a route or an area was partly the cause. Perhaps that high-speed dash in the dark onto the Beasts of Holm by the *Iolaire* had a similar touch of overconfidence. And, of course, many a lifeboat is called from its station to risk the lives of its crew to save yachtsmen who should have known better when sailing into danger in impossible conditions. The same reck-lessness and disregard of the weather also played a part in the great Eyemouth fishing disaster of 1881. But when it comes to wrong decisions to put to sea, perhaps the most tragic and costly in terms of life was the loss of HMS *Hampshire* in 1916, a complex tale full of mystery and con-spiracy theories that would have tested the imagination of the most talented writer of fiction.

More than 650 people lost their lives when the *Hampshire*, a coal-burning battlecruiser of 10,850 tons, built in 1905, plunged to the bottom of the Atlantic off the west coast of Orkney. But it was the name of one man that was on the lips of the men and women on the streets when the news of the naval disaster reached a population already reeling from loss of life in the muddy battles on mainland Europe: Field Marshal Horatio Herbert Kitchener.

These days, many people's awareness of Kitchener starts and ends with the famous recruiting poster of him heavily moustached and pointing out menacingly at the viewer with an unforgettable fierce face, with the words 'Wants You' under his image and in larger type the injunction 'Join Your Country's Army – God save the King'. But when he died aboard the *Hampshire,* which along with its crew had survived the Battle of Jutland – one of the last great sea battles of history, in which Britain lost three battleships to the Germans' one – Kitchener was already an iconic figure.

Born in County Kerry in Ireland, he had risen to the highest positions in the British Army and was familiar to the British public through his exploits in the Boer War and the Franco-Prussian War and as Commander-in-Chief in India for seven years. In more recent years, his reputation has been put under critical scrutiny, including debate about his sexuality, with varying conclusions. Even in the months before his death, controversy swirled around him. Despite his fame and position there were those in high places who were critical. Indeed, days before his death, when still in London, he was questioned in the Commons about his running of the war and his success or otherwise in the procurement of rifles and other weapons for the army. But a vote of censure failed and instead he was given a vote of thanks for his candour with his political opponents and his efforts to arm the troops.

As Secretary of State for War he was at the height of his political and military power when he set forth for Russia on his final fatal mission. On Sunday, 4 June 1916 he and a group of officials met at King's Cross station in London for the long overnight rail journey to Thurso in the far north of Scotland. So, when he went to Scrabster harbour, close by Thurso, en route to Scapa Flow and onwards to St Petersburg via Archangel on a high-level, supposedly secret diplomatic mission it can be assumed he was in a positive frame of mind.

At Scrabster he boarded the HMS *Royal Oak* for the short sea crossing to Scapa Flow and the *Hampshire*, which was under the command of Captain H.J. Savill. On arrival at Scapa he had lunch with Admiral Sir John Jellicoe, Commander-in-Chief of the Grand Fleet, on board his flagship HMS *Iron Duke*. No doubt at this they discussed the route to be taken and almost certainly a bad decision was made. The destination was Archangel and the meteorological 'experts' of the day were reporting a heavy gale blowing from the north-east. Some reports say there was talk of delaying the departure but that Kitchener himself insisted on sailing. But the weather had a trick or two up its sleeve.

With the reported winds, it had seemed a good idea to route *Hampshire* and its escorts up the west coast of Orkney, where there would be more shelter than on the east coast exposed to the gale, though that was normally the route used. It was thought that a route more out into the Atlantic would allow *Hampshire*, which had a top speed of more than 20 knots, to use that speed in the lee of the storm to dodge any U-boats prowling the area looking for targets. What was not taken into account was that the escorting destroyers simply could not keep up in the huge seas with the mighty cruiser and even though *Hampshire* dropped her speed to 15 knots they were in difficulty, eventually dropping even further back.

This move was authorised by Captain Savill reluctantly, but he had to accept that, unable to keep up with the ship they were supposed to be protecting, they were useless in the circumstance. This happened a short time into the voyage, at 6.30 p.m., which posed the question: should the mission have left the shelter of Scapa Flow that day in the first place? Bad decision-making? Should Kitchener have listened to sense?

Another factor was that just before the *Hampshire* sailed, the wind had swung round from north-east to north-west, the worst possible change, as it now threatened the cruiser from the open Atlantic. Weather experts nowadays will tell you that this is predictable in such a storm. But the danger of the cyclone effect did not seem to occur to the Met experts that night in 1916.

There was a further complication. The areas off Orkney were clearly ideal for German U-boats to patrol, threatening the heavy sea traffic going to Russia and other ships heading for North America by this route. And when not able, for weather or other reasons, to hunt down the British and unleash their torpedoes, they could be used for mine laying. There was a minesweeping operation, but, of course, you can never be sure you have made an area 100 per cent safe.

Captain Savill, however, seemed to be unaware before he sailed of the most recent U-boat intrusion in the area when *U-75*, under the command of Lieutenant Kurt Beitzen, had without detection laid no fewer than twenty-two mines. This lack of information could have been caused by a failure of naval intelligence or poor bureaucracy, but the fact was that reports of the U-boat activity simply never got to Savill. There are also theories that an attempt at deliberate misinformation by British Naval Intelligence alerted the Germans to the new route and led to mines being laid in some numbers in the right place to hit the cruiser. In addition, the navy did not seem to have considered that the weather in the past few days had hindered any attempts by them at minesweeping. With the virtue of hindsight it looks as if it would have been prudent to delay the sailing. Clearly Kitchener should have listened.

In the end, the danger of hitting a mine was greatly enhanced by the timing of the voyage and the opportunity the poor weather conditions had given the enemy U-boats. The *Hampshire* did hit a mine, some say two, and was fatally damaged. And once that happened, the death of Kitchener and most of the men on board was inevitable. Only twelve of the 662 aboard survived, mostly low-ranking sailors, which tends to support the theory that the captain and the officers, as is traditional and expected, stayed on board to the end. Indeed, there are reports of Kitchener himself standing on deck as a watery grave beckoned, erect and talking to his men as he waited for death. Out in the wild Atlantic that night, there was little hope of rescue for those who chose to risk the lifeboats or to simply jump into the stormy waters.

But not everyone had even the chance to make a choice. If you were down below, especially near the boiler room where the mine struck, you were killed outright, or burned and scalded, or simply trapped as the vessel went down near Marwick Head at 7.40 p.m. It took only around twenty minutes from the time it hit the mine until the cruiser was under the waves. The weather was appalling and there was little time to launch the lifeboats, though some rafts were manhandled into the water. Reports at the time said that around seventy sailors got into those rafts, but as they drifted towards the shore in the dark and in stormy seas the cold took its toll and with hands frozen and all hope gone the survivors dropped off to drown.

The minutes and hours after the ship hit the mine were a mixture of confusion, panic and incompetence, some of it verging on the unbelievable. Obviously you get no warning when you hit a mine, but it is still strange that in the time between the explosion and the sinking no rockets were fired by the crew and, even more odd, no wireless SOS was sent. In fact, a territorial on Birsey who, from his lookout post, saw a navy ship in distress first raised the alarm. Telegrams were then sent to the naval base at Longhope. What happened next was astonishing. There was no immediate launch of boats on a rescue mission. Instead there was debate about whether it was a cruiser or a battlecruiser, whatever difference that would make, and confusion about whether the ship had just been damaged by the explosion or had sunk. Eventually rescue craft from the navy base headed to sea almost two hours after the *Hampshire* had hit the mine.

If that was bad enough, there was worse to come. The navy refused the islanders permission to launch the Stromness lifeboat. And islanders were warned to stay away from the cliffs near the area of Marwick Head. Apparently the reason for this counterproductive edict was the fact that the navy feared the island had become a base for groups of Irish and German saboteurs and there was concern about the security of Lord Kitchener and his party should the men on the mission have reached the shore. If this is the case, it is remarkable, as lack of security about the mission before it set out from Scapa was later criticised. Kitchener sailed in June, but in the month before the voyage it was discussed openly in the capitals of Europe. No undercover work by ace spymasters was required to learn of the pending trip.

So much for the basic known facts of the fate of the *Hampshire*. But immediately the news reached the general public a storm of conspiracy theories began to batter against its perception of what had happened out in the Atlantic and why. Before looking at some of the outrageous explanations put forward, it might be appropriate to first of all point out the effect of Kitchener's death. The modern parallels are the assassination of John F. Kennedy and the mysterious death of Princess Diana in Paris. For years after the drowning of Kitchener, when folk talked of it they would have recalled where they were and what they were doing at the time. It was a moment of history etched on the memory of millions.

Such was the strength of the legend of Kitchener; in fact, many a man and woman in the street seriously thought it could lead to Britain losing the war. Many simply believed that he was still alive. Somewhere. In the years after the death of Elvis Presley, you could hardly open a tabloid without reading that the musical icon had been spotted in a supermarket in Surbiton or San Francisco. In Kitchener's case there were wild rumours that he had been seen leaving the ship in a dinghy (in huge Atlantic rollers!) or that islanders had spotted a high-ranking soldier come ashore. The nation was so shocked by his death and wracked by such tall tales that some credulous citizens were sure that the Secretary for War would soon be back at the helm, leading his army against the Hun.

Other bizarre theories gripped the imagination of news-paper readers: a popular one was to pin the blame on the Irish for the death of the war hero and the humiliation of the navy, who had failed to look after him. Much was made of the fact that the *Hampshire* had been to Belfast for work to be done on her not long before the fatal voyage. Had time bombs been set? Or had stowaways hidden in secret places, only to emerge with Kitchener on board? Everyone was jumping on a bandwagon. Even in Germany, men claiming that they were spies and it was they who had sunk the *Hampshire* published a number of books after the war.

This fervid atmosphere of claim and counter-claim is easy to understand when you think of the Kennedy assassination, and the longevity of some of the crackpot theories around it despite a government investigation. Here officials in Britain were so perturbed by the growing industry in false claims that ten years after the sinking they produced a White Paper to dismiss at least some of them.

Most of the rumours were started by folk with a political axe to grind. Some, and these were the most imaginative, were the products of clever crooks on the make. There are two classic examples. The first is the story of hoaxer Frank Power, who claimed in the same year that the White Paper came out that he had the body of the missing war hero. His claims were published in a long-forgotten paper called the *Sunday Referee*. The paper later disowned the story, but his inventive tale was that a Norwegian fisherman had found the body of Kitchener. Power then said he had headed for Norway to reclaim the body and some versions of the story say that en route and on return a gullible public figure donated money for this enterprise. It was said, too, that

118

when the coffin appeared in Britain, where it was to have a proper burial and a state funeral at St Paul's, that crowds lined the streets and people doffed their hats as it passed by. Inventive and imaginative as Power seems to have been, he was not prescient enough to realise that before the burial the authorities in England would have wanted to inspect the body. When this was finally done – by the legendary pathologist Sir Bernard Spilsbury – before the arranged burial, the coffin was found to be weighted down with tar. No body. Power was an all-round shady character who had been writing rather bizarre stories on the *Hampshire* for years, and he was interviewed by the police, who inexplicably believed his story that it was all done in good faith and that he was as surprised as anyone when the coffin turned out to be empty.

A tall tale, but not as bizarre as the claims of Frederick (Fritz) Duquesne, a South African who had fought for the Boers and claimed that he had attempted to assassinate Kitchener in Cape Town but had failed. The motive for this attack was that he hated what the British had done to his country. Not a man to give up too easily, Duquesne came forward with a cracker. He had, he claimed, joined Kitchener's entourage in Scotland, prior to the sailing, posing as a Russian duke, Boris Zakrevsky. This dangerous character said that when on the *Hampshire* he had signalled a German U-boat, which obligingly torpedoed the cruiser and he had been rescued by the sub, and later awarded the Iron Cross for his trouble.

It all seems bonkers, but Duquesne was a man of some ability. After the First World War he moved to the United States, where he was arrested for a humble run-of-the-mill insurance fraud, a crime not in the same class as his earlier

119

outlandish claims, but he managed to escape. His next move was more spectacular. In the Second World War, he ran a German spy ring in the United States but was caught by the FBI. This was no small operation but a huge ring involving thirty-three agents. Indeed, when, along with his men, he was caught, J. Edgar Hoover claimed it was the largest spy round-up in history. Huge sentences were handed down in 1941 to the traitorous group who had done important work for the Germans in the area of sabotage and intelligence. Duquesne got eighteen years and found himself in the infamous Leavenworth Penitentiary in Kansas, a long way from his birthplace in Cape Colony. This was no soft touch, as the inmates took every opportunity they could find to torture and batter the traitor. He did not complete his sentence but was released some years early because of illness and he died in New York.

Other conspiracies put forward were perhaps less spectacular but more sinister. For example, Lord Alfred Douglas saw a connection between Kitchener's death and the Battle of Jutland, which had preceded it, and with Winston Churchill and an alleged Jewish conspiracy. This resulted in Churchill winning a case for criminal libel and Alfred Douglas going to prison.

But there is yet another mystery of the *Hampshire* – did it have a cargo of gold bullion? In the years following 1916, the disaster was seldom far from the headlines. But a new dramatic twist emerged in a Berlin newspaper report in 1933 that said £10,000 in gold bars had been salvaged from the cruiser's strong room. It was a story that soon developed international legs and was picked up in the British and American newspapers. The British naval authorities said they knew nothing of the alleged salvage and that the ship, and presumably any money in it, was the property of the British Government.

A book in the 1950s – *Unlocking Adventure* by Charles Courtney – claimed that even more than £10,000 had been recovered in a diving expedition, which ended when one diver died. The site of the wreck off Marwick Head would be difficult to dive in because of strong currents, and some experts have questioned the possibility of this story being true. Nonetheless, there is circumstantial evidence from islanders that in the summer of 1933 an unknown ship was spotted in the area of the wreck. Courtney claimed this salvage operation was bankrolled by the German industrialists Krupps, and an arms dealer known as Basil Zaharoff.

It's yet another fascinating tale in the complex story of HMS *Hampshire*, but the fact is that the Bank of England and the Admiralty say that no bullion was on board. Why would there be?

Again, we run into conflicting theories. One that the money was to help the Russian war effort, the other that the gold was privately owned by the Romanov family. The fact is that when that mine – or perhaps torpedo – took the *Hampshire* down, it also created one of the most enduring of sea mysteries and one that you suspect will continue to run.

Stand on Marwick Head, beside the tower built by public subscription to honour the memory of Lord Kitchener, and gaze out to the stormy waters of the Atlantic and ponder the mystery. But don't stay too long – you might come up with yet another theory.

9

THE INGLORIOUS END OF
THE MIGHTY *HOOD*

Growing up on Clydeside, it was impossible not to be interested in the great ships fashioned in the yards on both sides of Scotland's most famous river's banks. As a schoolboy I had a collection of postcards and small books, given to me by my dad, on the great liners and warships, which carried the accolade 'Clyde built' across the oceans as a byword of quality. The legendary names all featured in grainy black and white: *City of Paris*, *Aquitania*, the beautiful Canadian Pacific *Empress* liners, the Queens, *Mary* and *Elizabeth*, and many more. But my favourite in one well-thumbed booklet was an impressive shot of the battlecruiser HMS *Hood* at full speed off Scotland. It was an unforgettable boyhood image for me as, low in the water, she ploughed through the ocean swells at high speed. It was many years later before I realised that impressive low profile was a result of poor design and botched alterations that left the warship vulnerable to plunging enemy shells.

Built at John Brown's Yard in Clydebank, the *Hood* had its original design altered because of the navy's experience, losing three battleships at the Battle of Jutland. Blame for the loss of these ships was apportioned by some to lack of proper armour on the decks, making them vulnerable to shells coming in from a height and penetrating to magazines and ammunition storage areas. So thousands of tons of armour were added to the *Hood* at a cost to weight, speed and manoeuvrability. It also meant, of course, that the *Hood* went to war much heavier than had been designed and resulted in her sitting much lower in the water than most of her contemporaries. She was what sailors call a 'wet' ship. At full speed in rough weather, seawater would flow along her quarterdeck. The water even got into mess decks and living quarters through the ventilation shafts. She was often sarcastically referred to as 'the largest submarine in the navy'.

All this made for a spectacular sight, at a full speed of more than 20 knots. No wonder, as a sea-struck young Glasgow boy, I was fascinated by the 'Mighty Hood'. This was in an era when thousands worked in the legendary yards – Denny, Alexander Stephen and Son, Fairfield, Barclay Curle, Connell, Yarrow, Brown's and more. Workers in these yards and other yards, and their families, were proud of what they had created and liked to follow the careers of their ships long after they had skidded down the slips in a roar of sound, dragging huge braking chains, into the murky waters of the great river. The city's newspapers catered for their readers' hunger for nautical news with daily shipping columns. Reporters devoted their careers to chronicling what was being built in the yards and what was sailing up the Clyde, and the departures of the great ships down-river to trade in the oceans of the world. The shipping correspondent was a man of stature. Even in the city centre you could see masts and flags, and smell the steam, oil and smoke. There was an air of glamour to these great days of the Clyde.

The *Hood* was born in Clydebank, but ended her career dramatically in the Atlantic near Iceland, after sailing from Scapa Flow in Orkney. If you make that journey to Marwick Head and the Kitchener memorial, gaze north to see the *Hood*'s last resting place over the horizon. There is another link with the *Hampshire* – as she sank with hundreds of lives lost in 1916, Brown's at Clydebank was ringing to the sound of steel being fashioned into a warship that was, for a time, the most feared in the world.

The *Hood* was supposed to be one of a class of four new ships to counter the threat of the German Navy's heavily armed and armoured battlecruisers. But in the years after the First World War, the arms race was changing fast and only the *Hood* was completed. One of the reasons for this was the fact that some in authority thought the money would be better spent on merchant ships, to take the place of those sunk by U-boats. Another factor was that the Germans were running a huge programme of submarine-building. There was great competition for resources. The *Hood* was, at 860 feet long, larger than her predecessors of the Renown-class. At near enough 50,000 tons she was a big warship driven by steam turbines, which in sea trials in 1920 allowed her to make a remarkable 32 knots. The speed was supposed to be a vital part of her design and was admired by the US Navy, who regarded her as a 'fast battleship' rather than a battlecruiser. Subsequent refits and redesigns over the years reduced her top speed but, despite the thousands of tons of steel added to her armour, she was still vulnerable to plunging shells coming in from height.

She was launched on 22 August 1918 by the widow of Rear Admiral Sir Horace Hood, a great-great-grandson of Admiral Samuel Hood after whom the *Hood* was named. The flaws in her design, which were to emerge in the last great shooting wars of the battleship era, were of little importance in the 1930s, when she cruised the world showing the flag for Britain's naval power. In those days, in harbours in the Mediterranean and around the world, tiptop gin and tonics for the VIPs attending functions on board were one of the first concerns. Apart from the Mediterranean, there were cruises to Brazil and the West Indies. But the highlight of those years was a world cruise via the Panama Canal in 1923. The motive for this flamboyant exercise was to remind the dominions of the might of our sea power and maybe, too, to encourage them to provide some money to continue that state of affairs. She returned in the spring of 1924 after visiting South Africa, India, Australia, New Zealand, Canada, the United States and some other far-flung colonies.

Amid all this sunshine and blue skies, there was one darker incident. When on her way to the Mediterranean for yet another cruise, she was rammed by the battlecruiser *Renown*. Though the damage was minor – a huge dent and some damage to a propeller – it did the image of the navy's competence no good at all. Nor did the various court martials that followed.

As the start of hostilities approached in 1939, she was beginning to show her age. All that propaganda-cruising was taxing on the ship, if not the crew. With her career coming to what was to be an ignominious end, she should have been having much modernisation work attended to, but instead the war meant there was no time to take her out of service. The wear and tear meant she could not maintain her designed speed.

When the shooting started, she was used principally in patrolling the area of Iceland and the Faroe Islands. The job was to protect convoys and to intercept German blockade runners trying to break out into the Atlantic. In one incident she was attacked by a Junkers Ju 88 bomber and sustained some damage that, though repaired, added to her dire mechanical condition. After this, there was a spell in southern waters before being sent to Rosyth, along with *Nelson* and *Rodney*, as there were real fears of a German invasion across the North Sea. When that threat receded, she ended up being based in Scapa Flow in May 1941.

The end was coming close. Naval intelligence had indicated that *Bismarck* was heading out into the Atlantic and a group of ships, including the *Hood* and the battleship *Prince of Wales,* was sent out to cut them off. On 23 May, the British spotted the *Bismarck* and its companion *Prinz Eugen* between Greenland and Iceland. A battle between these, the mightiest ships of the warring nations, began.

It was not to last long. Contemporary reports say that the *Hood* opened fire around dawn on the *Prinz Eugen*. Both German ships fired back, both at the *Hood*. The first hit is thought to have come from the *Prinz Eugen,* hitting the *Hood* between her funnels. This started a large fire and five minutes later, when the *Hood* was on a sharp change of course to position her guns, she was hit again, this time by one of five salvos fired by *Bismarck*. A gigantic jet of flame from the *Hood* leapt skywards from near the mainmast and there was a huge explosion. Debris showered down on the fatally wounded ship. She sank in just three minutes. 1,415 men died and only three sailors survived to be picked up by the destroyer *Electra*. This was a greater loss of life than on the *Hampshire*.

It was a devastating blow to Britain's war effort. The *Hood* was an iconic symbol of its naval power. And it was gone in just a few minutes. The news came to the nation in a terse and rather odd communiqué from the Admiralty. It read:

> *British naval forces intercepted early this morning off the coast of Greenland by German naval forces, including the battleship* Bismarck. *The enemy were attacked and during the ensuing action HMS* Hood *(Captain R Kerr, C.B.E. R.N.) wearing the flag of Vice-Admiral L.F. Holland, C.B received an unlucky hit in the magazine and blew up. The* Bismarck *has received damage and the pursuit of the enemy continues. It is feared there will be few survivors from HMS* Hood.

These few words gave millions the shock of the war. It was said that it was decoded again and again in hope that it was some mistake. It was almost impossible for the man and woman in the street to conceive how something like this had happened to the mighty *Hood*. Unlucky perhaps, but most probably factually wrong. The cause of such a massive death toll and such a naval humiliation was much more complex than 'unlucky' suggests. From this distance in time it is astonishing that the *Hood*'s companion, the *Prince of Wales*, had to disengage the attack, despite hitting the *Bismarck* three times, because of mechanical failures in her turrets and guns. The German warship was, however, forced to run for safety and repairs in occupied France. She was spotted and sunk by the British on 24 May, but that is another story – or film!

The usual inquires began and the first, just a fortnight after the sinking, concluded that the probable cause of the loss was 'the penetration of one or more of the shells at a range of 16,500 yards, resulting in an explosion of one or more of the aft magazines'. This quick inquiry was criticised on several counts. One naval construction expert came up with the theory that the explosion of her own torpedoes had destroyed the ship. Another inquiry followed, but it supported the findings of the first. Over the years there have been many other theories put forward, the wildest being that it was a malfunction of one of the ship's own guns that caused it to take in water so fast that the back of the vessel broke, quickly taking it down with the bows almost vertical. However, recent diving expeditions seem to confirm that the magazines did explode. It is all rather academic when placed against the reality of the death toll.

The awesome sight of the huge bows standing vertical and sinking into the depths was witnessed by the last of the three survivors, Ted Briggs, who died in 2008. His testimony is poignant and moving. At the time when he lost his ship and his crewmates, he was an eighteen-year-old officers' messenger. More than fifty years later he said: 'we had taken them by surprise and fired about half a dozen salvoes before she replied. But when she did, her gunnery was excellent. The third salvo hit us at the base of the main mast, which caused a fire. Then we were hit just above the compass platform, which caused some bodies to fall down. I saw one officer with no face and no hands.' Ted Briggs went on to say that he first saw the great ship as a boy of twelve and, from that moment on, he wanted to serve on her. He wasn't alone. The iconic ship was a great recruiting tool for the navy. The glamour of the world tours got huge newspaper coverage and the *Hood* was splashed across the press in picture after picture in the years before the Second World War. She projected power and prestige, and created what turned out to be a deadly fascination in this island nation.

10

LIFE-SAVERS LOST AND ISLANDS IN GRIEF

In this voyage around Scotland, the next move is north-east to the Pentland Firth (though some would say it is more accurate to call it a 'straight or straights'). This is a location with a history and a future – both are a result of the remarkable tides in the area. The waters between Orkney and the mainland contain some of the fastest moving tidal streams in the world, with surges of up to 30 kilometres-an-hour thundering in from the Atlantic on one side and the North Sea on the other, often thrust along with extra force from frequent gales. This is a constant danger, even to modern vessels with radar and satnav, and it must be navigated with great care. Nautical almanacs and suchlike contain dozens of pages of advice and warnings – you do not sail safely hereabouts without much forward planning, good luck and good weather. But these very tides could hold a key to pushing Scotland into the front of the worldwide race to harness tidal power and produce cheap electricity.

Many experts in the field believe that this is the best place on the planet to develop the technologies involved in the production of tidal power. Indeed, Scotland's first minister Alex Salmond has gone as far as to say that the Pentland Firth has the capacity to become the Saudi Arabia of tidal power. Trials of generators are underway and in the next few years some further huge experimental trials will take place. It will be ironic if the same tides that cost hundreds of lives should in the end be an engine of prosperity for the area.

The Pentland Firth has been the scene of shipwrecks for hundreds of years, especially in the days before the lighthouse came into being. A combination of dangers comes into play when you look back into history. Orkney comprises of around seventy islands and the coastline is around 550 miles long. There are hundreds of miles of cliffs, but some of the islands are largely low-lying and hard to spot in poor visibility, particularly Sanday, and many of the wrecks occurred when vessels simply sailed into land that they could not see in fog, which can be frequent and heavy, or land obscured by sleet, snow or blinding rain. And voyagers had to handle all this in addition to the rip tides and whirlpools.

As far back as 1540, an author called Alexander Lindsay wrote: 'betwixt Dungisbe and Orkney there is great daunger causit by nepe tydis'. He then proceeded in *A Rutter of the Scottish Seas* to give advice on how to avoid the 'daunger' – advice that had little success, if you look at the number of shipwrecks. The weather and rocky coastline apart, another factor is that the Pentland Firth was for hundreds of years one of the busiest areas in Europe. In the days of sail, hundreds of cargo vessels made their way through it on voyages taking materials around Britain from west to east or vice versa, and it also was a major route connecting trade from Russia, Scandinavia and northern Europe to markets in the rest of the world. Even before such commercial activity, there are stories of shipwrecks in the area, including some on Shetland. The *Orkneyinga Saga* mentions Norse ships *Fifa* and *Hjolp* grounding on Shetland in 1148.

At times, various historians have compiled lists of sea disasters in the area, lists that name hundreds of ships. To illustrate the size of the problem, it can be pointed out that one such list looks at the year 1847, among others, and lists no less than eleven incidents. The destinations listed and the cargoes mentioned show the importance of the Firth as a sort of maritime 'motorway' round the north of Britain. For example, in August 'some lives were lost' when the *Britannia* heading for Belfast with rye-meal went down. August was a bad month that year. It also claimed *Triad* of Dundee, travelling from Leith to Skye, and *Canton*, a barque out of Hull for America (this time all hands were lost). Incidentally, the islanders made good use of debris, timber and suchlike, sometimes even food and drink, left on the beaches after wrecks to ease the hard life on those northern isles.

In another incident, this time in 1898, the sheer power of waves ripping though the Firth was demonstrated. A new large ship, the 9,000-ton *City of Manchester*, was en route from north-east England to St John, New Brunswick. Some say it was her maiden voyage, but other sources disagree. She was relatively new and state-of-the-art for long distance ocean voyaging. Yet in the Pentland Firth she met seas heavy enough to tear away part of her steering gear. With no steering, she 'threw down the hooks', as they say, but in those infamous tides they were carried away and failed to stop her being swept around, almost in circles, and in grave danger of hitting a rocky shore. Distress signals were sent out and the famous Longhope lifeboat – more of her later – answered the call. It was to be a remarkable rescue. The coxswain, Benjamin Stout, was a man of decision and told his crew he would try to save the ship as well as the crew. With great skill and bravery, he got within what looked like jumping distance from the ship and, in a huge acrobatic leap, crew member Bill Mowat managed to jump onto the ship's ladder. It was an exceptional leap and he landed so hard, it was said, that days later his boots had to be cut from his feet because they were so swollen by the impact. The remarkable Mr Mowat then took control, though how he did it is a mystery not explained in accounts of the incident, and the ship was saved.

This was a happy ending for the folk of Longhope and the owners and crew of the *City of Manchester*, but many years later the little settlement and its lifeboat were to feature in a poignant tragedy reported worldwide. The disaster of the lifeboat *TGB* was one of the worst in the history of lifeboats. Lifeboatmen in all parts of the world respond to a call for help without thought of their own safety. They know the risks, but saving lives at sea is what they are all about. It was the same for the men of Longhope, but there are few maritime incidents where the fates were more spectacularly reversed, or where a tragedy has such a dramatic effect on a small community.

In March 1969, only around thirty folk lived in the remote community of Brims. The loss of the local lifeboat took a man from every home, and many of the crew who died were related. The appalling nature of this was clear, even to city dwellers. In towns and large communities major accidents can take life, but the vast majority of people do not know those who die. It was different in Brims, where everyone knew everyone else. This particular sadness was, however, also felt in many parts of the world furth of the Orkneys. An appeal for aid for the families raised the remarkable sum of more than £100,000 in a mere few weeks. The fact that in this case the brave rescuers died and those they set out to save survived makes it one of the most poignant missions in lifeboat history.

The *TGB*'s most unnautical name reflected the fact that the money to build it – around £35,000 in 1962 – had been donated by a wealthy donor who wished to be anonymous. It had twin engines and was 47 feet in length, with a breadth of 13 feet and a draft of 4 foot 6 inches. A sturdy vessel. But of significance was the fact that this Watson-class boat was not self-righting. Nowadays, most lifeboats in service worldwide have the ability to right themselves after a capsize. This would have been very desirable in the *TGB*, destined to work in the Pentland Skerries in vile conditions when called out. In seven years' service, *TGB* took part in several rescues and saved a considerable number of lives. One of the most dramatic involved an Aberdeen trawler that came ashore, where all but five of the crew were rescued in an operation involving the use of a breeches buoy. However eventful and exciting such work was, the *TGB* did not make the global headlines until 17 March 1969.

As is most often the case, the call for help came by radio. The ship in difficulties was the Greek-owned Liberian registered *Irene*, which was en route to Norway from Granton, near Edinburgh. The night the call came to the men of Longhope was one of the wildest in living memory and the folk in the northern isles of Orkney and Shetland have more experience than most of such weather. Winds there have regularly been measured at 100 miles an hour and 'maelstrom' condition often recorded. But this was something special. Rain mixed with snow and in a force 9 gale, the waves were said to have reached 60 feet high off Orkney. For landlubbers, the only thing to give an idea of what it was like would be, I imagine, a viewing of that remarkable film *The Perfect Storm*, which was in cinemas a few years ago. Or perhaps a view of the 1998 Sydney Hobart ocean yacht race in which five boats sank and six yachtsmen died, an event much shown on TV newscasts. No on-board cameras were on-hand, however, when the *Irene*, with seventeen on board, was in real trouble off the east coast of the Orkneys.

Her crew's navigational ability raised some questions. In their radio plea for help they said she was eighteen miles off South Ronaldsay, but this was wildly wrong. Indeed, afterwards, many wondered how long she had been 'lost' in the gale. An inquiry after the disaster by Liberian authorities found that the crew had no real idea where she was and that she had been out of control and drifting for some time. But as her end neared, she was in fact only three miles off the east coast of Orkney. Apart from the radio call, the crew set off flares, which were seen by the inhabitants of South Ronaldsay, and by the time she actually did run aground on Grimness there were people on the shore ready to help. And help they did – the entire crew was saved after a line had been fired out to ship and a breeches buoy rigged. Those who staggered ashore were in a sorry state but alive. Meanwhile, the *TGB* was offshore in the nightmare waves searching for the *Irene*.

It had been around 7.30 p.m. on 17 March when the lifeboat secretary at Brims had been alerted by the coastguard that the *Irene* was in deep trouble. Despite the weather, the

135

TGB was launched and headed out to sea to help. A few minutes after nine she radioed the coastguards that she was one mile east of Swana. At 9.15 p.m. the *Irene* hit the shore and her positiion was given to *TGB* and acknowledged at 9.28 p.m. That was the last heard from the lifeboat crew. Around ten minutes later, the lightkeeper on the Pentland Skerries reported seeing her stern light as she battled through mountainous seas. Wick radio called at 10.10 p.m. but there was no reply. The calls searching for the missing lifeboat went out every five minutes. No reply. At 10.30 p.m., with still no reply, the coastguards were extremely worried. The Kirkwall lifeboat, the *Grace Paterson Ritchie*, a larger design at 70 feet, had also been launched after the distress calls from the freighter. She was asked to search an area from Grimness to a mile east of Old Head. They found nothing and had to run for shelter from the horrific conditions. Darkness had also fallen.

As dawn broke on 18 March, a huge sea search was mounted for the missing lifeboat amid a grim feeling that something had gone seriously wrong. Included in the search for the *TGB* were lifeboats from Kirkwall, Stronsay, Stromness and Thurso, a helicopter from RAF Lossiemouth and a Shackleton aircraft from RAF Kinloss. The worst fears of everyone involved came true at 1.40 p.m. when the Thurso lifeboat found the *TGB* capsized four miles from Tor Ness Point on Hoy. The upturned lifeboat was towed to Scrabster harbour with seven of the eight dead crew members still trapped inside the cabin. The eighth crew member, James Swanson, was missing.

The bodies were returned to a grieving Brims and a funeral service was held in Walls Old Parish Church. In August 1970, the Queen Mother unveiled an impressive bronze statue of a lifeboatman at the graves. The mariner is gazing out to sea. It is a moving reminder of the courage of the men of Brims, who for years before the disaster risked their lives to save others. A plaque on the statue says it all: 'Greater love has no man than this, that he lay down his life for his fellow men.'

This powerful piece of sculpture is well known and by now a tourist attraction on Orkney. Indeed, the lifeboat station is also a place of pilgrimage for those interested in the history of life-saving.

But the statue is not alone in marking a sea tragedy. The islands have been the scene of many wrecks down the years, as previously noted, but unlike the fate of the *TGB*, which was recorded in poignant detail and at length in the modern media, most are now forgotten. But there is another stone monument to be seen in these parts – a 40-foot-high tower located on the shore in the Mull Head area. It's a reminder of a disaster that took around 200 lives and is largely forgotten.

The ship involved was the *Crown*, which was dashed against the rocky shoreline at Scarva Taing. The tower is known as the Covenanters' Memorial. The men aboard who perished were fighters who had taken part in the battle of Bothwell Bridge in 1679. The Covenanters, fighting threats to Presbyterianism, had been badly beaten by the forces of the Duke of Monmouth and more than 1,000 were marched in pairs to Edinburgh to be held in horrific conditions in a part of Greyfriars Churchyard that had been converted into an open-air prison. The authorities lost patience with a rump of uncooperative prisoners and decided to transport them to slavery in the American Colonies. The actual transport was to be done in two ships chartered by an Edinburgh merchant, William Paterson, on the make and looking for a juicy profit by selling his passengers into slavery. But by the time the authorities ordered the prisoners to depart, only the *Crown* was available. The conditions in the makeshift Edinburgh prison had been horrendous but worse was to come for the men who were marched to Leith. They were all – more than 250 – crushed into a space barely suitable for half their number at most. Writer Roddy Simpson, in an article in the *Scots Magazine,* reported that one of the Covenanters, a James Corson from Kirkcudbright, wrote from the ship that: 'all the trouble they had met with since Bothwell was not to be compared to one day in their present circumstances; that their uneasiness was beyond words'.

The religious faith of these men was impressive. Corson said in his letter that 'they are near their port and heaven is open to them'. He died in the wreck, perhaps a mercy considering what an Atlantic voyage in such conditions, and a life in slavery in the colonies, would bring.

Apart from the delay in erecting the memorial, another intriguing part of this story is that, as is often the case after disasters, there is a conspiracy theory. Indeed, two in this case. One suggests that the *Crown* was not intended to reach her destination and that the dangerous route, passing the Orkneys in winter, was deliberately chosen. The normal route from Leith would have been to sail south and round Land's End out into the Atlantic. Whatever the reason, the doomed ship sailed north and anchored in Deer Sound to take on water. In a horrific winter storm, the terrified prisoners pleaded to be let ashore, but instead were kept below under locked hatches. The ship dragged its anchor and broke up on the rocks with great loss of life. Some did survive and there are stories of them marrying locals and staying in the islands. Others were recaptured and did, indeed, end up in slavery in the colonies.

A second conspiracy theory is that the evil Paterson wanted insurance money for the ship. Who knows? But looking back, it seems that the loss of the *Crown* and 200 souls was simply another case of Scotland's cruel sea claiming its victims.

In the case of the *TGB*, the memorial was erected swiftly. But for the victims of the *Crown* it took until 1888 for the tower in their memory to be built. As in the statue of the lone lifeboatman gazing out to sea, a plaque was attached to the stone. This one reads: 'For Christ, his Crown and Country. Erected by Public Subscriptions, August 1888, to the memory of 200 Covenanters who were taken prisoner at Bothwell Bridge and sentenced for transportation for life, but perished by Shipwreck near this spot on 10 December 1679.'

The reason for the delay seems to be that at the time the folk of the Orkneys were not sympathetic to the Covenanting cause and regarded the prisoners as rebels, though some of the victims were commemorated in their home areas. Gradually, however, Scotland as a whole became more sympathetic and a book published in 1883 suggested a memorial. The funds were donated and after the tower had been built enough cash was left for a small memorial in front of St Magnus Cathedral in Kirkwall.

This book is peppered with sad tales of the memorials to disasters, ancient and modern, and many plaques of remembrance are mentioned. But the story of the *Crown* has a special place in nautical history – it took 200 hundred years for it to be remembered and then it was in not one, but two, memorials.

There are many factors in every sea disaster, whether the loss of a fishing boat, a large car ferry or a naval vessel. Clearly, around Scotland's coast, gales, rip tides, uncharted rocks, reckless or bad seamanship, or simple bad luck are involved at various times in various combinations. With regard to loss of life, though, there is a constant – the temperature of the water itself. The word for it is cold. But it's a word that does not accurately define the danger. Reading *The Secret Life of Bletchley Park* by Sinclair McKay, one of many books on the Second World War codebreaking centre, I came across an interesting reference to the waters of the Firth of Clyde. The author mentions that a German U-boat (*U33*) was detected laying mines at the mouth of the Firth in February 1940. The minesweeper, HMS *Gleaner*, went on the attack, and after some hours successfully forced the U-boat to the surface, where 'its crew, stranded in the open, freezing waters, were forced to surrender'. On board the sub was an enigma code machine and in the pocket of one of the frozen submariners were three of the machine's code wheels. The crew had been given these wheels and told to dump them in the sea, to stop the navy getting its hands on them. But apparently not all the Nazi submariners obeyed the order.

This particular sub had a record of preying on unarmed fishing vessels, and on one occasion the commander was seen cackling in the conning tower and pointing to the plight of survivors struggling to escape from him, a nasty little anecdote on the wickedness of war. The capture of the wheels, however, was an important breakthrough for the Bletchley Park boffins in their battle to read the enemy's secret messages.

The Longhope disaster is still, of course, a powerful folk

memory in the Orkneys, though it has, sadly, to some extent, dropped out of public consciousness on the mainland. But there is a poignant reminder of the tragedy at Irvine on the Firth of Clyde at the Scottish Maritime Museum, which reopened after an excellent refurbishment in the spring of 2014. This is a place well worth a visit by anyone at all interested in our engineering and maritime heritage. The lifeboat *TGB*, from which the heroes of Orkney were swept to their death, is one of the most striking exhibits in a museum not many miles from Glasgow and Clydeside. The paint is fresh, the brass polished and it is a handsome vessel. Ironically, it looks strong and sturdy enough to tough out the roughest of weather. But it was one of the last of the non-self-righting lifeboats. And if it was not clear to anyone following the story of the failed rescue mission just how exceptional the weather was in that storm almost half a century ago, visitors to the museum are left in no doubt.

Under the blue painted bow there is a pedestal and a photograph of the crew. In oilskins, sou'westers and naval style caps, they gaze out, looking proud and competent: men who knew the sea well in sunshine and storm. But brave and skilled as they were, the gods decided to take their lives that fateful March day. In a low-key caption, it is quietly remarked that the freak wave that overturned *TGB* was thought to be 100 feet high. It is a fearsome observation to be read in the warm comfort of a huge, well-heated indoor space. It takes no great leap of imagination to think what it must have been like on the Pentland Firth, motoring to the aid of the stricken *Irene* in a deadly cold and howling March gale.

The *TGB* itself was recovered virtually undamaged. In the Orkneys, it had been launched thirty-four times and rescued twenty-four people. When it was restored to full service capability, it was naturally thought to have been insensitive to return it to the same station. It was instead sent to serve in Ireland, where it had a further forty-one call-outs and saved ninety-one lives. It 'retired' in 1979. In Irvine, it is one of the most striking exhibits and deservedly attracts much attention.

This book has looked at the toll taken by the cruel seas around our home coasts. But a saunter round the Maritime Museum reminds the visitor that Scots risked their lives in many foreign seas as well. One of the best sections in the museum honours the memory of the great days of the Clyde shipping lines, such as the Clan Line, the Ben Line, Donaldson, the Anchor Line and the Clyde Shipping Company. Colourful posters show the ships and list the exotic destinations: South and East Africa, Ceylon (as it was), India, Suez, the Red Sea, Aden, the Seychelles and, nearer home, the Mediterranean ports. Many of the men who ended up sailing around Scotland in ferries, fishing boats, Royal Naval vessels, pleasure steamers, coastal traders, lifeboats and tugs had had adventurous blue water careers before coming home to brave Scotland's storms.

A day at the Irvine museum is certainly time well spent for anyone with even a passing interest in our maritime heritage. Though, in its recent reincarnation it has lost one exhibit that reminded visitors of a tragedy at sea, costing four lives. This tragedy, unlike many of the incidents recounted in this book, was not weather-related. The fishing vessel *Antares*, out of Carradale, was lost on 22 November 1990 off the north of Arran, dragged under when its nets were snagged by a Royal Navy submarine. The sub was the 4,500-ton hunter-killer nuclear-powered HMS *Trenchant*.

The *Antares* was recovered from the depths after some early resistance by the navy. It emerged from the deep, largely undamaged, and ended up in Irvine, moored for public view at one of the jetties belonging to the museum. This was not thought appropriate by many Argyll people and, in particular, the families of the crew members. The men who died, and who will never be forgotten in Argyll, were Jamie Russell, William Martindale, Dugald John Campbell and Stewart Campbell. I was given a potent illustration of the effect on local people by a prominent Carradale man, Stuart Irvine and his wife Sylvia. Stuart has long had connections with the Argyll fishing industry and told me that there was a local tradition that on the arrival of a new boat, one bought by a Carradale man from other owners or a brand new vessel, the locals were invited aboard perhaps for tea and biscuits, or more often a wee dram, to toast a welcome to the new addition to the village's fleet. Those invited aboard often responded by taking a wee gift with them for the crew. Stuart and Sylvia, whose home overlooks the picturesque harbour, took some nautical mugs to the *Antares* – you know the sort of thing, skipper or mate or whatever emblazoned on the side of the colourful mug. It was a happy day.

After the salvaged *Antares* had gone on display in Ayrshire, the Irvines found themselves in the area and took a look at what was now a museum exhibit. It was an emotional moment. The mugs they had taken to the boat were still hanging from hooks in the dining area. The table was set. It was upsetting and seemed somehow not 'right' for visitors to invade the space in which the victims had lived. Many others with connections to the village and the families were unhappy about the *Antares* on show. Tourists who still flock to this attractive fishing village can, as people have

143

done for a century or so, stroll down to the pier to throw a line out in search of mackerel or simply watch the comings and goings of the fishermen making a living out on the waters after 'spoots' (razor fish), prawns or clams, as the locals call scallops. The views east over the Kilbrannan Sound to Arran and north up towards Loch Fyne are superb. Recently there has been more 'action' for the tourists to watch, as feed boats come and go to a new fish farm in the area, which has provided welcome employment at a time when the fishing boat numbers are in decline. Here the *Antares* and its crew will never be forgotten. Visitors to the old pier stop and read a plaque on the wall, remembering one of the blackest days in Scottish fishing history.

The loss of the *Antares* had an impact on the whole fishing industry off Scotland's west coast and resulted in many changes in the way the navy went about its work in waters dotted with yachts, ferries and fishing boats, all of which could be endangered by naval activity. The crew of the *Trenchant* took the blame for snagging the nets of the fishing boat going about its work on a calm clear night, unknowing of the danger. A report by the Marine Accident Investigating Branch reported directly that there had been 'a partial breakdown in the watch keeping structure and standards' on board the sub, producing a flurry of newspaper head- lines along the lines of 'Submarine crew blamed for sinking of *Antares'*, though, in the interest of fairness to the men of the sub's crew, it was the 'command team' rather than the ordinary seamen aboard who caused the tragedy. The report also said incorrect information from the *Trenchant* led to an eight-and-a-half-hour delay in mounting a search and rescue mission 'which may have contributed to the loss of life.'

144

The sub was taking part in the famous 'Perishers' training exercise for submariners on the verge of qualifying, for the right to have their own command. The course was, thanks to various newspaper features and TV documentaries, the most infamous exam in the country. The pressure of the final tests was immense and there is no doubt tension contributed to the tragedy. This was demonstrated by the report, which found that control of the sub passed from the *Trenchant*'s skipper to the captain of the command course and to the student being assessed, who was referred to in the report as the duty captain. The collision with the *Antares'* nets happened when one duty captain was about to hand over to another student. It was said surface vessels in the area were being tracked by the sub's sonar. There is always the whiff of suspicion that such reports end up as a whitewash. The report into this incident may have been confusing at times about the role of individuals, but it at least did not dodge the fact that the navy was to blame. But there is still local anger that the navy did not do enough to punish those whose actions, or lack of actions, caused the disaster.

The report said 'the command team on *Trenchant* had no clear appreciation of the surface contacts held on sonar during the period between the completion of the exercise and the collision'. It also said that the sub's crew 'did not fully appreciate that there were two vessels within sonar contact relevant to the collision going in opposite directions'. Too much attention was said to have been given to the Royal Navy vessel *Charybdis,* which was taking part in the 'Perishers' course exercise. In addition, it was found that the concentration of the duty captain was 'impaired due to his conversation with the next duty captain in the minutes before the collision'. The command team of *Trenchant* was

home port of Kilkeel. Ian Bruce said in his *Herald* piece: 'sixteen other fishermen have disappeared in mysterious circumstances in the same area over the previous ten years. No one has ever admitted liability. Most were probably the victims of freak waves but some, almost inevitably, must have succumbed to the heavy NATO and Soviet submarine traffic beneath them.'

A US Navy court of inquiry, aware of the breach of UK safety rules, decided the *Sturgeon* 'had not operated in a prudent manner' and disciplined her commanding officer. The Royal Navy reacted to the sinking of the *Antares* with new rules and new cooperation between the subs and the fishing industry. It must be said that they do work, but there is no room for complacency when you remember that today there are still nuclear subs patrolling off Scotland, and some pass close to major conurbations on their way to duties in the deep Atlantic. It is sobering to think that despite all the top-secret high technology contained in vessels such as HMS *Astute*, one of the Royal Navy's new class of nuclear submarine, it could still, in 2010, manage to run aground near the considerable lump of land known as the Isle of Skye. It had to be hauled off a sandy spit in full sight of rubber-neckers on the Skye Bridge. Some saw humour in this humiliation of the navy. Others, more savvy on the history of naval accidents, were less impressed.

11

THE HELL THAT WAS PIPER ALPHA

Perhaps of all the disasters that have taken place in the cruel sea around this little country, one of the most recent is the most deeply embedded in the public's consciousness: the huge loss of life on the oil and gas rig Piper Alpha in July 1988. This was the UK oil industry's worst offshore disaster.

The bald facts show the enormity of what happened when the hunt for black gold under the seabed by multinational corporations went wrong. Of 220 crew members, 165 died, as did two of the crew of the standby vessel *Sandhaven*. This disaster and other fatal accidents – mostly involving helicopters ferrying crews to and from the rigs in testing weather conditions – are a black spot in the history of the industry. Like mining onshore, danger is an everyday reality for everyone who lives out on the huge rigs, anchored on the seabed and towering above waves that reach 70 feet in height in the storms that sweep the area. Oil and gas has brought previously undreamed of wealth to Scotland, and the north-east in particular, but the price is high. And not just for the folk who live in the area – the big wages attract thousands to spend weeks out on the North Sea, on the rigs or servicing them, or working the dangerous trade of saturation diving to maintain the pumps and pipelines under the sea. A spell on the rigs became something of a rite of passage for adventurous young Scots. In days gone by, the whaling industry operating out of the north-east of Scotland held a similar attraction for young Scots with adventure in their blood – even Sir Arthur Conan Doyle made a voyage to Greenland as a ship's doctor. But the list of those who died on Piper Alpha and in other accidents out in the oilfields contain names of people from every corner of the country.

The rigs and the wealth from them were a long-time coming. It was not until the sixties that exploration showed that massive reserves of oil and gas lay under the sea miles out into the deep waters east and north of the coast. But, surprisingly, Scotland had an oil industry way back in the 1850s. This was largely the result of James 'Paraffin' Young, a chemist who devised a way of extracting oil from some types of coal and oil shale. The history books credit him with the creation of the world's first oil refinery. Though it has to be said it was a pygmy in scale compared to the refineries set up to process the crude flowing out of the North Sea today. And it did not claim lives.

In 1988, Piper Alpha had been in production for more than a decade. It was owned by Occidental Petroleum at the time of the accident. It was originally designed as an oil production platform, 300 metres high with four main working sections, which had firewalls to separate them. They had been built in two units: one in Scotland and one in France. The sections had been joined in Ardersier. It had a helideck and an automatic fire fighting system, with electric and diesel pumps to pump seawater into outbreaks, a system that was not in use at the time of the accident. The installation was later converted to handle gas as well as oil, and was part of a maze of connecting pipelines taking energy to Flotta on Orkney.

The 1988 accident, which happened around 120 miles out in the North Sea, was caused by a number of factors, including human error and the sheer difficulty and complexity of getting oil and gas from under the seabed and piping it ashore. Ten years before Piper Alpha turned into a deadly fireball, there had been a warning of what could happen when the largest offshore blowout in the world at the time took place in the Norwegian section of the North Sea.

The Ekofisk Bravo platform blowout was largely due to the failure of a safety valve. A huge uncontrolled release of oil and gas occurred but some lucky factors meant that there was no great damage to the environment. Much of the oil evaporated largely because of unusually high temperatures at the site, and rough seas helped break up the oil before it could do much damage. More importantly, all the personnel on the platform escaped without injury in lifeboats, a method of escape facilitated by the fact that there was no fire. It took a week to cap the well, which spewed oil and gas high into the air in an expensive and spectacular demonstration of what can go wrong in an oilfield. The official inquiry concluded that the major factor was a series of human errors, including misleading paperwork, poor planning and 'improper well control'. What would have happened if the escaping oil and gas had caught fire is frightening to contemplate. But if it was a wake-up call to the industry, few seemed to be doing any serious listening and, ten years later, the reports of human error and bad planning had a familiar ring to industry insiders. You suspect that in the early years the imperative in the mind of many at the top of the industry was greed for black gold. The oil industry attracts risk takers.

When the news of what was happening on Piper Alpha hit the front pages and dominated the airways of Scotland, it came as a shock. The danger in the North Sea was recognised by a news aware population who had been used to death and disaster in their newspapers, especially in mining and fishing communities, but this was something else: hell at sea on a huge scale. It came out of the blue, an unexpected disaster that pushed the country into something like collective shock. No one who was around at the time can forget the sensational pictures of the burning rig on television or on the front pages. It took the full horror into the homes of millions. It was shortly before 12 a.m. on a calm night out in the North Sea when the first explosions were heard and reported. A massive rescue operation swung into action, involving thirty helicopters (the area was full of them for ferrying duties), twenty-five boats and seven NATO warships. Helicopters were like buses to the oil industry, and even in Aberdeen and Peterhead today the almost constant buzz of them in the air going about their business strikes the visitor. In the hours after these first explosions, sixty-seven men were rescued from the inferno on the platform. Flames and smoke burst high into the air in frightening patterns as the massive steel structure broke apart.

For the next few days, the papers were full of stories of the victims, the bereaved and heart-breaking accounts of what had happened. The Queen, the prime minister, politicians and public figures of all kinds offered heartfelt

151

sympathy to victims and their families. The stories of the injured survivors were particularly dramatic and horrifying. Readers of the papers at the time were much emotionally affected by these personal accounts of men who had lost so many friends and colleagues. Working out at sea on a rig helps forge lifelong friendships.

The first-hand accounts are just as affecting to the modern reader. In July 2013, on the twenty-fifth anniversary of the disaster, there was a service of remembrance in the Memorial Garden in Aberdeen's Hazlehead Park. The minster remarked on how emotional that service had been, particularly when a piper played a lament. There was no shortage of tears. One of the survivors who attended the service, Roy Thompson, told the BBC how he had escaped from the blaze by jumping into the sea far below: 'My mind was made up for me, my feet were on fire and so was my boiler suit. There was no thought to it, if you are on fire, you jump.' That was the reality. In the days after the accident, and for years after, there were many other survivors who told similar stories and who carry their injuries, mental and physical, with them for life.

The harrowing accounts of the accident have not lost any potency over the years. What survivors were telling reporters and interviewers still has the power of contemporary newspaper reports. In the immediate aftermath, the tabloids and broadsheets were filled, page after page, with first-person stories of what it was like by those lucky enough not to have been killed by the immediate explosion, those able to jump into the sea in hope of being plucked to safety by the armada of rescue boats that surrounded the burning wreckage of the platform. The heat of the fireball fuelled by thousands of tons of escaping gas and oil made the deck red-hot in areas. The waters around the base of the rig steamed. There were patches of burning oil floating on the sea. And those whose life jackets kept them afloat long enough to be picked up saw a scene from hell, as the light from the burning fuel lit up the sky, and clouds of dense black smoke rolled hundreds of feet into the air. Roy Thompson's account of jumping more than 100 feet down into the waves was mirrored in many other stories.

The lifeboats had been destroyed in the initial explosion and for many jumping was the only option, but it, too, had its horrors: one survivor told of being forced deep under and coming to the surface in water so horrifically hot that he immediately and instinctively dived under again to seek escape from the heat. Others found themselves floating surrounded by men already dead. A few of the crew managed to run down some stairs to a position nearer the water to jump. Some slid down pipes in the scramble to escape the flames and certain death. Others slipped down knotted ropes that had been used by divers to get to the water and left to help anyone who could use them. Men were trapped as parts of the rig began to break up after the explosion of a pipeline connecting Piper Alpha to the Claymore platform. These unlucky men could hear metal tearing itself apart as they shook hands in the face of death. Those eyewitness stories of survivors were vivid. So, too, was the grief of the bereaved. Public opinion and public memories turn over fast and many tragic stories are swiftly forgotten to be replaced by another, but the anguish of those left behind goes on. In a powerful newspaper column, the popular TV presenter Jackie Bird told of years when she was a neighbour of a woman who had lost her man in the fireball. Jackie sympathised greatly with this woman and her family, who did not spend a day in the rest of her life without thinking of that July night her world exploded as dramatically as Piper Alpha did. Jackie summed it up perceptively: 'all the compensation money in the world couldn't dent the hole left in her life and that of her children. Her wounds were as deep as any of the injured and they never healed.'

Part of the fascination with the Piper Alpha story was that this was, as noted, different from readers' expectations: it was unfamiliar ground. Plane and train crashes, mayhem on foggy motorways were a staple of the news pages. This was new, a disaster unlike any other, hell miles out to sea on a static platform heavily populated by workers of many trades, from canteen assistants to painters and engineers, scaffolders and divers.

Another reason that Piper Alpha stays so graphically in the memory of Scots is that it coincided with a revolution in the newspapers the folk of this country devour with an enthusiasm not equalled elsewhere. This was the year full-colour reproduction on newsprint was introduced. The old days of black and white were being replaced with colour reproduction of high quality. I worked for the Herald Group at that time and we were jealous of the tabloids who had stolen a march on the more conventional broadsheets by adopting the new processes first. Until that unforgettable night of horror, no colour news photograph had appeared in the august pages of *The Herald*. Change did not happen fast in this place and the paper had even been among the last to sweep adverts off the front page to be replaced with news. But the owners had finally invested in equipment to take it into the new era and the production staff were involved in dummy runs and trials of all kinds involving colour, but up to that moment it had not been used for real. Then the photographs began to emerge from the North Sea.

The editor Arnold Kemp, an unforgettable man and a brave journalist who could inspire remarkable loyalty and affection among his troops – not something you could say about all editors – was shown the first dramatic shots by his picture desk. They wanted them in the paper, some technical folk thought we weren't ready yet. Arnold led from the front and he took an immediate decision. In his long career he had often taken on top-level politicians and the establishment, and he had a taste for risk-taking. *The Herald*'s technical experts had not finished their trials, but that image was going on the front page. It did. And it worked. Readers saw the scene as never before. Few would forget it and I suspect the shock of seeing that blazing rig in full colour helped those who fought in the aftermath, to investigate and pursue every avenue to prevent similar disasters in the future. It helped the survivors and their families in the convoluted and difficult lengthy fight against the oil companies for decent compensation. This was no easy task and took years, with some of those seeking justice feeling that it was as difficult to extract fairness from multinationals as it was to get the oil and gas to the surface.

As survivors, in hospital or at home, attempted to come to terms with what had happened to the rig and their lives, the fires still burned as if hell itself was rising from the depths of the sea to the surface. The new problem was how to put it out. Most cinemagoers knew the answer – send for Red Adair. And the oil companies did just that. Those who watched the film *Hellfighters*, with John Wayne playing Adair in a fictionalised account of the legendary firefighter's life, would have seen a lot of footage of land-based oil fires.

155

And it was certainly true that Adair made his name in American oilfield blazes, though the Texan made international headlines as far back as 1962 when he snuffed out a pillar of flame, known as the Devil's cigarette lighter, in the Sahara. This was some fire: the flames blazed from November until April and leapt 450 feet into the air.

But he was no stranger to the North Sea, as it was he and his crew, including that other legendary firefighter 'Boots' Hansen, who had capped the blowout at Ekofisk Bravo. Boots and another Adair associate, Ed 'Coots' Matthews, went on to start their own oil firefighting firm known as 'Boots and Coots'. Red Adair had designed the specialised vessel *Tharos*, which took part in the life-saving events immediately after the Piper Alpha explosion. When called in, he knew he had big problems, as the rig's legs extended 400 feet down and miles of pipelines were spilling crude onto the blaze. He directed operations from *Tharos*. Water at 70,000 gallons a minute was sprayed onto the fire and debris, some bits weighing tons, cut away to facilitate an approach to the well head. All this was done in the worst weather in the area for years, but in the best Hollywood traditions the job was done.

With the flames snuffed out, one chapter in the saga closed. The next was to find out how it happened and what could be done to prevent a repetition. That took a long time – a year – to establish. The inquiry under Lord Cullen came up with findings that mirrored much said after Ekofisk Bravo – findings not properly acted on. Cullen found that the errors in maintenance were the main cause, though there were others. The work was carried out on two important pumps and a safety valve at the same time. The safety valve was removed from one pump for maintenance and a remaining pipe temporarily sealed as the work could not be completed by the day shift. A night crew started work on an alternate pump, astonishingly unaware of what the day shift had done. The night crew turned on a pump and the temporarily sealed pump could not handle the pressure. It exploded and the resultant fire was then intensified by the failure to close a flow of gas from the Tartan platform. The automatic fire-fighting system had been switched off, as divers were working underwater before the incident. It all came from poor work by the owners in not having fail-safe procedures.

No one was ever prosecuted, something that would be unthinkable today. So sloppy was the operation of Piper Alpha that Lord Cullen was able to make no less than 106 recommendations, all of which were accepted by the government and the industry. The major recommendation was to emphasise the need for UK offshore installations to have a detailed written safety plan looking at installation design, major hazards and the protection of the workforce should a problem escalate into an accident. All of this did not make the North Sea a safe place to work – incidents still occur – but certainly the Cullen Inquiry made it safer than it had been. The memory of that sickening July night out in the North Sea must hover over the shoulders of anyone in the oil industry concerned with safety. So far there has thankfully been no other occurrence of that magnitude. But the Deep Water Horizon disaster in the Gulf of Mexico in 2010 shows that even in the modern era of oil extraction the threat of disaster is there.

But, of course, even such valuable work as that done by the Cullen Inquiry could not remove the other major danger in the North Sea: that of accidents involving the helicopters ferrying crews out to the platforms.

12

STEAM, SPEED, STEEL AND
THE SILVERY TAY

After researching the Tay Bridge disaster of the night of 28 December 1879, when a train travelling from Wormit to Dundee toppled into the icy waters of the river, one contemporary quotation stuck in my mind. A witness at the court of inquiry set up in the aftermath of the incident which killed everyone on board, testified that despite having lived in the area for almost thirty years, he had never seen anything like the storm that night. He called it a 'hurricane', as bad as 'a typhoon he had seen in the China Sea'. Meteorological detail was not then as precise as now, but the wind speed had been around 71 mph in Glasgow – even higher in gusts – though no reliable figures were available for Dundee. It has been said that the gale, estimated at 10/11 on the Beaufort scale, was blowing down the Tay estuary, striking the almost new bridge at right angles. The fascination of this, one of the worst engineering failures in British history, an event that shocked the country and the engineering community world-wide, continues to this day. Recently Met experts re-examining all the historical date have estimated that gusts hurling themselves into the bridge reached 80 mph. It was no ordinary storm.

But the exceptional wind was not the real reason or the only reason for the calamity. The seeds of death and despair to be visited on the folk of Scotland's east coast can be traced back to 1871, when the need for a crossing near where the Tay meets the North Sea was first recognised. The new bridge was to be almost two miles long, the largest rail bridge in the world at that time. It was to be an engineering marvel, a giant state-of-the-art demonstration of the bridge designers' mastery of steel and stone. It did not turn out that way. The 'Tay typhoon' saw to that. But for the first nineteen months of its life, it was, indeed, a source of wonder – a brief success. It cut the journey time from Dundee to London by hours. It largely took away the need for weather-dependent passenger ferries across the Tay and helped move valuable coal around the country. Queen Victoria used it on her journeys to Balmoral Castle. No doubt impressed, she knighted its designer Thomas Bouch, who was showered with fame and made a considerable fortune. It took six years and around £300,000 to build, a massive sum for the time. Bouch was also the man selected to design the even grander Forth rail bridge then planned.

When the trains started running in 1878, the public perception was that it was initially a great success. Bouch used a lattice of girders supported by cast-iron columns or stone pillars in most of his bridges, which meant they tended to look slender and vulnerable, which in the case of the Tay Bridge turned out to be so true – especially the steelwork above the level of the track. Crossing the Tay on the new bridge, which opened in 1887, you can still see the piers that supported the high girders under which the trains ran.

But even before the heavy locomotive and six-carriage trains would run filled with passengers, there were hints of what was to come. Painters and joiners, working on the bridge as it was being finished ready to enter full service, had noticed considerable movement when trains passed, sometimes an up-and-down motion, and at other times a lateral shift. It was claimed that when a train passed under the girders at the south end, the north end shook. The speed of the train seemed to affect the degree of 'shaking', which you might have thought would have caused serious concern. The artisans working on the bridge had little chance to voice any worries, but there were others in high places with doubts.

Ex-Provost William Robertson had, typically of those who made good in the 'city of jute, jam and journalism' (Dundee's epithet), a house in douce Newport-on-Tay just across the estuary from the city's docks and factories, a place to enjoy tranquil days in pleasant surroundings. The new bridge would have seemed a boon to him, ending the time-consuming ferry journeys across the Tay, especially in wild weather. But right from the start, this prominent local politi-cian had some concerns. So much so that, though he had been one of the first to buy a season ticket, he was soon using the railway only for one-way journeys and preferred the ferry for the other direction. It seems remarkable but it is recorded that the reason for this seemingly idiosyncratic decision was concern about safety. He felt the north-bound trains passed through the lattice of high girders too fast, cre-ating vibrations that he at least felt unhappy about. He must have been a bit of a railway anorak, as well as a successful politician, since he often used a stopwatch to time journeys. He also became a bit of thorn in the flesh for the stationmaster at Dundee, who seemed to have done little about the complaints other than speak to the drivers.

But it was a fact that the north-bound trains did often travel faster than those going south because they were often held up by expresses and tried to make up time on the bridge. Speed apart, there was something of a question mark over maintenance, which was the responsibility of the North British Railway Company, who had retained Thomas Bouch to supervise the good health of the bridge over the years his bridge was expected to be in use. Bouch made another bad decision when he chose a man who had worked with him on building the bridge to be his bridge inspector. This fellow was a bricklayer, not an engineer. Again, not much was done about reports that said all was not well with the structure.

The old-fashioned railway 'block' system using batons was the chosen method to control the access of trains from each end to the single line across the icy waters. In this system, the train allowed on the bridge had to have a baton, and there was only one, in order to prevent head-on collisions. It was just before 7.15 p.m. when a train, from Burntisland for Dundee, slowed at the signal cabin to pick up the baton that allowed it onto the track and out under the high girders, which were lashed and buffeted by the gale, one of the worst to hit Scotland for many years. But you have to assume that, minutes from death, the passengers were not concerned – had the bridge not been designed and built by a master of the craft? And the fact that it was the festive season could also have contributed a certain feeling of relaxation to those on board.

Everything changed in seconds. The first hint of disaster came when some in the signal cabin saw sparks 200 yards out on the bridge, coming from the wheels of the train. There were witnesses who said they saw one sudden flash of light followed by total darkness. The train failed to appear at the north end. The unthinkable had happened. The locomotive, its crew and the carriages and passengers had disappeared 88 feet into the waters of the Tay, wrapped around by the failing high girders. There was no escape. Contemporary paintings of the scene show small vessels in high seas, lashed by the gale and searching in vain and at great danger to themselves for survivors. The mighty new Tay Bridge was no more.

How many died is still a subject of controversy. Many accounts suggest the total was seventy-five, but there can be no certainty about this. Debris and bodies were still being found washed ashore up and down the Tay estuary for months. However, all the known deaths – fifty-nine – were registered in Dundee. The list is long and a surprising number of the victims were relatively young. Perhaps this is because it is more likely that young folk would be travelling at the festive period. And, as in all tragedies, the details of the deceased are poignant. Eliza Smart, just twenty-four and a 'table maid' from Kingsbarns, was the niece of an Ann Cruickshank and fiancée of George Johnston, both of whom also died. David Cunningham was only seventeen and a mason, as was Robert Fowlis, twenty. Elizabeth Hendry Brown, working as a 'tobacco spinner' was just fourteen when she was hurled to her death. An iron turner, a farmer, a ploughman, a mechanic: the list of ordinary folk whose lives were cut short makes grim reading.

The wild wind contributed to the cause of the fall of the bridge, but in retrospect it seems that this was an accident waiting to happen. Various inquiries found that the power of the wind had not been properly allowed for in Bouch's calculations. Design defects were not the only cause – mistakes in construction and maintenance were also identified. Any notion of letting Bouch loose on the design of the new Forth Bridge was dropped. Sir Thomas Bouch, knighted by Queen Victoria, died only a year and a half after the sword touched his shoulder. He was a broken man. Interestingly, the only real survivor of this debacle was the locomotive itself, which was dragged from the deep, repaired and returned to service.

The attention of the man many call the world's worst poet, William Topaz McGonagall, so-called 'poet and tragedian', has helped lengthen the memory of the Tay Bridge disaster. Dreadful poet or not, his words can still be found today and he is in the folk memory of many Scots. I remember well my father, something of a bibliophile, reading aloud to me 'The Tay Bridge Disaster' with humorous relish. To those unaware of this poet, who wrote more than 200 pieces and who survived rotten fish being thrown at him at public recitals, a few lines from his best known piece give a flavour of his much imitated style:

> *The train into the girders came*
> *And loud the wind did roar*
> *A flash is seen, the Bridge is broke*
> *The train is heard no more*
> *The bridge is down, the bridge is down*
> *In words of terror spread*
> *The train is gone, its living freight*
> *Are numbered with the dead*

You can only take so much of this stuff, but there is no doubt that in small doses it is entertaining, so much so that some folk hold 'McGonagall suppers' with a dram or two in the style of a Burns Supper. It is the only spot of humour in a sad tale of deadly human error. The disaster in 1879 resulted in his most famous poem and his name is forever linked with what, 'in McGonagall speak', is always the 'Silvery Tay'. A pity that McGonagall was not around for the centenary of the disaster: he might have taken inspiration from the superstitions of modern day folk. In 1979, British Rail commissioned a special train to take railway buffs across the new rail bridge at the exact time of the crossing of the 5.20 p.m. from Burntisland to Dundee 100 years previously. There was a memorial service and a wreath was cast into the waters. But there was speculation that some of the more superstitious would get off the train at the south end of the bridge, just in case lightning did strike twice. In the end, all went to plan.

The death certificates of the victims provoke an interesting thought: the cause of death is listed as drowning. But, of course, many might have received fatal injuries in the fall or, as the records mention, died of hypothermia – no one will ever know. But there is no doubt that the icy water of the Tay estuary in mid-winter played a role, as hypothermia did in other disasters discussed in this book. For example, writers on the sinking of HMS *Hampshire* and the death of Kitchener suggest that the mine that blew the warship up or the torpedo, depending on which theory you support wasn't the real cause of most deaths, it was being thrown into the ocean in sub-zero temperatures. The same applies in the case of the east coast fishing disasters to be chronicled later.

Of course, there are many factors in every sea disaster.

With regards to loss of life, though, there is that constant – the temperature of the water itself. The reference in an earlier chapter to the freezing waters of the Firth of Clyde and HMS *Gleaner* is dramatic, but even in February the temperature of the waters of the Firth of Clyde are hardly comparable with that of the Northern Isles, the fishing grounds off Iceland and even the North Sea. As a young man, I tended to have summer holidays in the pleasant East Lothian resort of North Berwick and a dip in the sea there was altogether different from day trips down the coast from my home in Glasgow's southside to places such as Troon. Various geography teachers had for years hammered into us the effect of the Gulf Stream on the west coast. The theory was splendidly confirmed by a dip on the Ayrshire coast: cold but still in summer 'alright once you were in', as they said. In North Berwick, it took real determination to crawl out from the shelter of the ubiquitous, in these less sophisticated days, canvas wind break and plunge into the much colder waters of the North Sea.

Prompted by the stories of what happened to the victims of the bridge disaster, I decided to find out more about hypothermia from one man who knows more than most about the effect of cruel cold seawater. He is Professor Nelson Norman of Aberdeen University, a world-renowned expert in remote health care. Nelson is an agreeable man of enormous energy who wears his great knowledge lightly and is entertaining company. He is the author of two remarkable books: *In Search of a Penguin's Egg* (a very readable account of his time as a surgeon in Antarctica) and *In Search of Remote Health Care* – the story of how the Scottish medical profession dealt with the challenges it faced after the discovery of North Sea oil. It moves on from the first

165

steps in supporting deep-sea divers to the foundation of a
new system of remote medicine that would be successfully
exported round the world. He told me much about the
danger in our cold seas:

*The sensation of cold on immersion is very variable and its
extent is determined by the protective response of shivering,
which produces heat by muscular activity. Those who have a
poor shivering response and thus do not feel the cold think they
are tough guys, but are, in fact, vulnerable because their temperature can fall quickly to dangerous levels while they are still
admiring the seagulls overhead. Dick Laws, director of the
British Antarctic Survey, used to enjoy a midday swim in
Antarctic waters and pull himself onto the ice with an ice axe.*

*Another hard man, Alex Cumming from Raasay, did the
same in the Antarctic and one day found that he was bleeding
when he emerged because the sea was about to freeze and contained spicules of ice! We are not all the same and survival in
cold sea can be more prolonged than many think if death does
not result from the injury caused by entering the water, the
inability to prevent aspiration of water in rough seas or cardiac
arrest following the shock of entering the water. There are thus
wide variations in response to cold and immersion in cold water,
but water is particularly dangerous since it conducts heat away
from the surface twenty-five times faster than air, which is a
poor conductor. Although the surface of the sea may be warmer
in summer, there is little difference in temperature lower down
and the North Sea remains at 8 degrees Celsius throughout the
year below the surface.*

*It is, however, a little warmer in the vicinity of the offshore
structures in the North Sea and this attracts fish – indeed a
North Sea diver has reported encounters with unusually large*

and rather fierce catfish. The face of the cruel seas of Scotland have changed in recent years, with the search for further sources of energy below the waves. This changed risk was shown most dramatically when the Piper Alpha platform blew up in 1988. Although there was huge loss of life, this could hardly be blamed on the sea and even those who perished in the sea at that time were probably killed by injuries sustained on entering the water. The industry has also seen big changes in rescue techniques, so that the lifeboat has largely been replaced by the helicopter. When the helicopter lands in water, however, it does not have the same ability to withstand the waves as a lifeboat, and tends to capsize very readily, making it necessary for offshore workers to be trained how to exit a capsized helicopter before proceeding offshore. Communications have also been greatly improved in recent times, so that help can be provided with greater expedition than in the past.

Nelson went on to make the interesting observation: 'As with most advances, this also has a downside and when a message was received in an offshore structure in the Shetland basin some years ago, from a trawler, that a crew member had been shot and required urgent medical attention, a young surgeon responded. He was on the structure at the time and although the helicopter captain stated that the weather was such that it was ill advised to attempt the journey the young surgeon persuaded him to make the attempt. The helicopter crashed, killing the pilot, his co-pilot, the surgeon and the experienced winch man. Subsequently, it was found that the problem was an air gun pellet in the trawler crewman's leg accidentally caused by himself when trying to shoot a seagull.

The emergence of the new type of lifeboat has also

required a new type of crew and so the winch man has emerged as an essential part of the crew. Someone has also to be lowered down on the end of the wire to seek the seafarer to be rescued. The late David Proctor, a well-known Aberdeen surgeon and an early exponent of this technique, described one of the problems, which was the twirling of the man on the end of the wire as he descended. The answer was simply to dip him into the sea!'

The experience of the oil industry has thrown up a whole series of questions on methods of escape from rigs in emergencies. Conventional lifeboats are of limited use, though they saved lives on Ekofisk Brava oilfield. Helicopters are the obvious answer, though they bring with them other risks, especially in high winds. Perhaps there is room for some new methods of emergency escape, like special types of floatation rafts that should be launched into the air from a damaged rig or perhaps a type of lifeboat that could be permanently moored to a rig. Over to the boffins . . .

13

FAILING CHINOOKS AND
FALLING SUPER PUMAS

There is no doubt that working on an oil rig is a dangerous way of life. The history of the developments of the offshore fields in the North Sea turns up a rather shocking fact: very many lives have been lost in the simple act of oilmen and women *getting* to their work. Civil aviation is now so highly controlled and safety conscious that hardly any of the millions of passengers who walk down the walkways to enter a big jet to cross oceans and continents give a thought to 'danger'. They are more likely to be concerned about the quality of inflight meals and entertainment that awaits them when shown to a comfy armchair.

But now, after almost half a century of exploiting the black gold under the seas round this island, it is upsetting to record that there is an entirely different culture when it comes to flying over the North Sea in a craft without wings and relying on rotors to keep it in the air. It is astonishing, after all these years and numerous accidents, that, in 2014, you can stand on an airport runway admiring the glistening paint job on a ferry helicopter, listening to the thump of rotors cutting through the air, smelling hot oil and aviation fuel and the sense of fear among the passenger setting out for another spell on a rig. It shouldn't be that way after countless crashes, countless inquiries and countless claims that 'It won't happen again.' Yet, that is the reality.

I spoke to an industry veteran about what it was like to go to work by helicopter. Ray Bulloch is a man with a taste for high-speed motorbikes and underwater diving of all sorts, including dangerous saturation diving. Incidentally his love of bikes and leather, which now tends to be indulged in European trips to watch the stars of the world's racetracks, was and is shared by many an oil worker. A big Kawasaki or Suzuki is ideal for a fast blast up the east coast to Aberdeen or Peterhead after a break back in Glasgow or wherever. In his day, Ray preferred a replica Manx Norton, expensive wheels designed for the Isle of Man TT, but affordable to a North Sea saturation diver. The one thing the oil giants could not be accused of was running a low wage economy – divers and rig workers made a lot of money, though as young men they knew how to spend it. I asked Ray over a pint that old cliché question of interviewers: 'What is the job really like?' He answered, 'How much time have you got?' Later he produced the following account that does indeed give the reader a taste of the experience:

What can you say about helicopters? Call them 'Choppers', 'Paraffin Budgies', and 'Whirlybirds' – whatever you like – they're still noisy, cold and uncomfortable. They vary and some are better than others; however, they have become the transport workhorse for offshore installation personnel, and for good reasons.

Their arrival and departure on any offshore installation never goes unnoticed and is always commented on, whether you're getting on it, or I should say hoping to get on it, because you're never sure until you're strapped in and off, or just counting the number of times it'll come and go before you are getting on it.

The first time I was in a helicopter, in the early seventies, I found it quite exhilarating, and even though that exhilaration waned, it never entirely disappeared. That may well be due to the attitude towards safety in those days, which, compared to modern practices, was very lax. That relatively laissez-faire attitude engendered a cosy 'get a window seat and peer out of the window' type feeling, which bitter experience was later to change. In the early days, you just turned up and got on (some passengers even with a hangover and certainly worse for wear from the night before); none of the stringent safety measures which apply now were in operation. These days they won't even allow you on if you're overweight.

The novelty of helicopter flight would give way to a resignation that we would have to put up with the noise and discomfort of what could well be a long flight. Conversation was all but impossible and dozing or reading was the easiest way to pass the time. Flying from onshore, the view from the window, if you had one, would be of the heliport falling away below you and the experience of rising over the surrounding countryside or urban area, depending on where you were flying from. The edge of a city like Aberdeen or from a more tropical or desert location, they would all eventually give way to the vast expanse of the ocean. I remember reading somewhere that the Earth is a 'rocky little planet', however, it's hard to believe that when you fly over many miles and miles of water for such a long time.

When you're on an offshore installation it has an aura of power, of being solid and immovable, however when you're flying towards it on a helicopter and see it from the air, set in the context of the ocean, it looks so insignificant and you can readily understand why some of the platforms are lost to the sea they stand in. It gives you perspective. A minority of passengers, however, find the helicopter flight harrowing and are very nervous before and during the flight and, I suppose, given that helicopters can and do fail, they have a point. Most people believe, of course, that it'll never happen to them and being at the time a saturation diver, I'm sure I believed it even more so.

All of the above is of course weather-dependent, as helicopters are susceptible to all sorts of weather delays. 'WOW' (Waiting On Weather) used to be the usual term. If you were offshore, you could be 'fogged in', stuck on the installation until the weather cleared. If you were offshore and had been counting how many 'get ups' until it was your 'get up and go', you were constantly scanning the weather and when on your crew change day a WOW notice appears, your heart sinks, especially if it's an occasion when there is something special you want to attend to onshore. Not everyone felt the same, though. Some guys want the extra money and don't mind being 'fogged in'; for them it's 'money mist.'

Even worse, imagine it's a couple of days to Christmas and your crew change day has come and gone, you're praying for the weather to clear just enough to let the chopper land. You get told by the diving superintendent that the chopper's on its way and to go and get changed and packed. You go and you're packed in literally two minutes because you've been 95 per cent packed and ready for a week. You've sprinted up to the radio control room and you're waiting impatiently for the 'budgie' to land, which you hear it is about to do, when, at the very last minute, in walks some oil company person and they take your place. It's not their crew change day for another day or so but they're not taking any chances with the weather, so they're pulling *rank and taking your place and they're off early for Christmas. You're stuck until 'whenever', which is what Control usually tells you if you make an enquiry about the next chopper. It happens!*

It's the opposite when you're still ashore and 'WOW'ed'; then, hopefully, you're staying in a good hotel and getting paid for the privilege, though in my experience it's more often the former than the latter! However, for all the bad points and disappointments of offshore helicopter travel, it's hard to see any other practical way of delivering offshore personnel to and from installations. Ship-to-rig transfer via the 'Billy Pugh' is not for the faint hearted. It may sound odd, but I rather enjoyed it – but that'll be the 'it'll never happen to me' attitude again.

Ray added an interesting footnote on recent changes, which are a remarkable contrast to the 'turn up and go' ethos of the old days. Now you need proof that you have been scheduled for a visit to an offshore location. If you are going offshore, the following is compulsory:

Valid passport or identity card;

Valid medical (offshore) certificate;

Successfully completed basic Introduction to Offshore Safety course and Emergency Response;

Training (0.5a) including Helicopter Underwater Escape Training (HUET), or: Basic safety certificate (such as VCA, MIST, or another equivalent certificate issued in another country);

You are not allowed to bring hazardous substances, alcoholic beverages, narcotic drugs or arms of any kind onto the offshore platform;

Your luggage will be checked for such items.

On arrival at your offshore destination:

> *Unfasten your 4-point harness after arrival when prompted by the crew or HLO (Helicopter Landing Officer).*
> *Never open the door of the helicopter yourself, always let the crew or HLO do that.*
> *The HDA (Helideck Assistant) will unload your luggage and place it next to the helicopter.*
> *When prompted by the HLO, exit the helicopter and pick up your luggage.*
> *Freight will be unloaded and taken off the helideck by the HDA.*
> *Leave the helideck as instructed by the HLO.*
> *As soon as you are below deck, you can take off your life jacket and hand it to waiting passengers or the HDA.*
> *Always first report to the radio or control room, which is signposted, possibly only with arrows.*
> *You will subsequently be given video instructions regarding health, safety, and environment (HSE). You are under obligation to adhere to these instructions.*
> *Also make sure you are familiar with and abide by safety instructions and the code of conduct for the platform.*

It is a comprehensive list and recent accidents have led to an even more serious attitude to safety, but you suspect that in the future, despite all the good intensions of the authorities, it could happen again. The history of North Sea helicopter ferry flights is littered with accounts of what went wrong and good intentions that never seemed quite enough. Initially, the public was not particularly aware of the situation but any complacency was quickly swept away by a series of headline-grabbing accidents. Perhaps the most significant of these in the early days was when a Boeing 234LR Chinook plunged into the sea on approach to Sumburgh airport in the Shetlands on 6 November 1986. Forty-seven passengers, including the crew, were on board and only two survived.

On the face of it, the Chinook looked an ideal vehicle for serving the rigs. A tandem-rotor twin engine medium lift helicopter, it had been in service with the RAF for four years before this accident. The primary design was for military applications and it was remarkably successful in this role, being considered rugged and reliable. During the Falklands War, there were reports that one Chinook had carried eighty fully equipped troops on a mission. Even more impressive is the claim that during the Gulf War one aircraft transported 110 Iraqi prisoners of war. But even the military record of this legendary 'whirly bird' is flawed. In June 1994, an RAF aircraft was taking a group of twenty-five British intelligence experts and a crew of four from Belfast to Inverness for a conference when it came down in poor visibility on the Mull of Kintyre. No one survived. Controversy and intrigue went on for years as to the cause. The crew were initially unfairly blamed, but many experts believed they were scapegoats and that the disaster had other causes. Rumblings of all sorts went on, including accusations of sabotage. Eventually that harsh decision on the pilots by the authorities was overturned and the crew was cleared. But what really happened is still far from clear. This was the RAF's worst disaster since the Second World War. It is a murky story, which will perhaps have some surprises still to come.

But all this was years into the future after Scotland heard of the Sumburgh disaster. The civilian version of the

Chinook had, like its military equivalents, a reputation as a workhorse. The details of the final hours of this particular Chinook demonstrate that well. It had originally operated out of Aberdeen airport but a few days before the crash had moved to Sumburgh to fly a shuttle service to the Brent oil field. Its first flight that day had been delayed by an oil leak, but that was repaired and it left the islands at around 9 a.m., to visit three platforms with freight and passengers. After a mere hour and a half, it took off from the Brent Platform C to head home. Its height for most of the journey was around 2,500 feet, but as the airport came into view it was cleared to descend to 1,000 feet. The intention was to land on Runway 24. But at around 4.5 miles out, the airwaves went silent.

As the crash was happening, a coastguard search-and-rescue helicopter had taken off from Sumburgh and its crew spotted life rafts in the sea. One survivor was seen clinging to a fair-sized bit of floating wreckage. The crew managed to winch him to safety and as they did they saw another survivor amid a group of floating bodies and he, too, was plucked to safety. Despite desperate searching, no more survivors were found. Early the next morning, a search for the sunken wreckage commenced with a diving support vessel, but it struggled to hold its position at the site because of rough seas and powerful currents. Fortunately another vessel, Shell Expro's *Stadive*, soon arrived on the scene and it, a semi-submersible, was able to handle the conditions well enough to recover the cockpit voice recorder, some of the fuselage, rotors, rotor heads and control systems, which were shipped to the mainland for accident investigators to examine. The *Stadive* also managed to recover all the bodies of the victims bar one.

The cockpit voice recorder revealed that the crew had

noticed a rise in the noise heard on the flight deck, followed by an ominous loud bang. This was no doubt the sound of the rotor blades colliding when they lost synchronisation. The official report said the accident was caused by this happening, owing to the failure of a 'bevel ring gear' in the forward transmission, which had been modified. The underlying blame was put on the 'inadequacy of a previously accepted test programme and the failure of a stringent inspection programme'.

The usual raft of recommendations to prevent a similar disaster followed. Basically, there was to be much tighter inspections control on modified components. A review of the procedures regarding Automatically Deployable Location Transmitters was to be reviewed, as the beacon on the Chinook failed to work when it suffered impact damage. This was the swansong of Chinooks in the North Sea oil industry. They were withdrawn and sold to be used in other parts of the world, utilising their heavy lift capability, but not licensed for passengers. The military, however, continued to use them. The oil industry took the decision that the Chinooks were too large for offshore supply work, something that anyone who had seen one of these noisy giants at an air show, or perhaps parked at an RAF base, might have realised before lives were lost. Mechanical failure was to blame for this accident, but when you see film of a huge Chinook landing on a tiny platform in a storm, it is obvious that only the great skill of the pilots prevented many another disaster.

The other great controversial air shuttle bus to the rigs to force its name onto the front pages of Scotland's newspapers is the Super Puma. It has had a chequered career of major incidents and loss of lives. But, occasionally, it has been at the centre of a good news story and Bristow's Flight 56c between Aberdeen and the Brae Alpha rig back in mid-winter 1995 was one such tale. The difference between life and death on this occasion was largely due to pilot skill.

The commander of the copter, Cedric Roberts, was massively experienced, with almost 10,000 flying hours in his logbook, and the man in the right-hand seat, Lionel Sole, was likewise a chopper veteran who had been flying with Bristow for five years. On a routine trip, the Super Puma flew into bad weather and was struck by lightning. The bolt damaged the tail rotor and although the aircraft managed to stagger along for a few minutes, eventually the rotor failed completely and the pilots had to make an emergency rotation onto the rough sea. This was done so skilfully that all eighteen on board (sixteen passengers and two crew) were able to exit the aircraft onto a life raft to be rescued. The investigation found fault with the design of the rotors, making them prone to damage by lightning strikes. It is not surprising that half a century of oil and gas exploration and extraction, which meant that at times there were almost 300 rigs out at sea to be serviced, has led to a great many accidents. But that brush with death on Flight 56c was not the only lucky escape.

Seven years before, a Sikorsky S-61N was forced to ditch when travelling from a drilling rig 70 miles offshore. All passengers and crew – thirteen people – were saved. On that occasion, luck was with them, as the accident occurred in almost perfect weather conditions. Helicopters can land in the sea, but whether occupants can survive the weather and sea conditions is the main factor between life and death. In a similar accident to that which occurred to the S-61N some years later, twelve men died of hypothermia, that deadly factor in the waters round Scotland. This crash occurred in December, when the sea was at its coldest.

Oil industry accidents are too numerous for all of them to be discussed in detail, but one curious statistic emerges; up until the 1990s the accident rates in the Norwegian and the Scottish sectors were roughly similar, but from then on the safety record of the British fields dropped behind that of the Scandinavians. I have seen no solid evidence of any one reason for this odd statistic. But, maybe, some would point to the Super Puma and its record. Though to be fair, the Norwegians also use this type.

Earlier in this chapter, I made a rather tabloid reference to the 'smell of fear' around the departure of a Super Puma on a mission to the rigs. My language was perhaps a tad lurid but it spelled out a truth. In more considered terms Tony Osborne, writing in *Aviation Weekly & Space Technology*, observed in relation to the most recent accident in 2013 that 'it spurred an unprecedented social media campaign against the use of the Super Puma family of aircraft in the North Sea. The various accidents involving this type also had a dramatic effect on oil worker confidence in helicopter operations.' Not surprising, as it was the fourth accident in five years.

Tony Osborne, a respected figure in the industry, went on to point out yet again that we cannot operate offshore without helicopter support. Civil Aviation Authority figures suggest that currently UK-based helicopters fly to and from around 230 fixed platforms and up to 100 mobile helidecks. More than a million passengers are transported each year.

At this point, a look at the history of the controversial Super Puma is appropriate. It goes a long way back. The maiden flight was in 1978, though this was in a military version. Super Pumas were made down the years by Aerospatiale, Eurocopter and Airbus. That it was a commercial success is demonstrated by the fact that in 2005 almost 600 of the different variants had been delivered. And it was considered particularly suitable for use by the oil giants working in the North Sea. But, nonetheless, there were a number of early fatal accidents, not all in the Scottish sector, and in one incident in Scandinavian waters twelve people were killed. It is of significance that 'a catastrophic main gearbox failure' was blamed.

A crash in 2009 off Aberdeenshire killed sixteen people and again the words 'catastrophic failure' cropped up, this time in 'the main rotor gearbox module'. A fatal accident inquiry took place in Aberdeen and lasted six weeks. It was presided over by Sheriff Principal Derek Pyle.

What caused the gearbox to fail? A fatigue crack was discovered, though its origin was not determined. In addition, a rogue metallic particle was also detected. The inquiry report said that: 'the possibility of a material defect in the planet gear or damage due to the presence of foreign debris could not be discounted'. The helicopter operators Bond admitted maintenance and inspection failures, especially not adhering to written down procedures to be followed when a metal particle was found. There were also communications failures causing misunderstandings between manufacturer and operator. Mr Pyle observed that on the evidence it was not proved that if any or all of these failures had not occurred, the accident would not have occurred, but that it still remained a possibility. The inquiry's report was perceptive when it observed: 'the traditional means by which helicopter safety is ensured is by way of rigorous maintenance procedures. Helicopter manufacturers should consider whether future research and development should focus on whether alternative metals or other materials can be developed to reduce, or eliminate the risk of spalling in helicopter gearboxes, and thereby lessen the dependence on maintenance procedures as the primary method of ensuring safety.'

This was good advice to the industry, but it was not any kind of magic bullet to speedily make travelling to work on a rig by Super Puma safer. Indeed, that was in the future and not the immediate future either. There was another Super Puma accident in 2013 that claimed four lives and in its aftermath there were all sorts of new initiatives suggested. Workers in the oil industry had, naturally, taking into account the Super Puma's history, already developed a reluctance to travel in this particular vehicle. The story of G-WNSB was the final straw for many. It led to reported confrontations where workers were wary to the point of refusing to board the aircraft and were brusquely told there was no alternative: if you did not want to take the risk, you could not work offshore. Rough talk, especially to a workforce that had lost friends and colleagues, and who were largely well aware of the history of the Super Puma.

This particular crash had a familiar ring. The aircraft was returning from the Borgsten Dolphin semi-submersible with nineteen on board and heading for Sumburgh to take on fuel, en route to Aberdeen, when a mere 1.5 miles or so from the field it plunged with little warning from the sky into the sea. There was no chance of a controlled landing. An interim report six days after the accident said the black box had been recovered, and that there was evidence that the chopper was upright and intact when it hit the water. But it overturned, filled with water and drifted towards the shore in mist and heavy seas. The four who died were Duncan Munro from Bishop Auckland, County Durham; George Allison from Winchester; Gary McCrossan from Inverness; and the first woman to be killed in a chopper accident in the North Sea, Sarah Darnley from Elgin. The loss of life could have been greater had the accident happened further out at sea, the nearness to the shore making the rescue work easier. The wreckage was pushed by heavy seas and a strong tide onto nearby rocks. The full story of what happened to G-WNSB is still not clear almost a year after the accident.

According to survivors, tragedy struck so fast there was no time for passengers to brace themselves for impact. But there was already some anxiety felt by those on board. One of the survivors, Paul Smart of Hull, told his local paper that on the approach to Sumburgh 'the pilot said ten minutes to landing but that ten minutes became fifteen then twenty and we were looking at each other'. Mr Smart said that there was a clicking noise like a bone breaking and the helicopter fell out of the sky. Amid panic as the copter filled with water, he managed to get a window open and get out. Others escaped the same way.

Paul Smart was wearing a survival suit designed to aid floatation and to act against icy water, but it had been torn on his exit from the wreck. He also reported that the strobe light, torch and personal location beacon on his life jacket were not working. He spent forty minutes in the water before a rescue helicopter winched him to safety.

In the midst of tragedy, there is always a human side. Onshore, Paul Smart phoned his wife and said he had been in a bit of an accident and she asked what had he done to the car, but when the television was turned on, she realised how lucky he had been. For four other families there was no such happy ending. The nightmare of losing a loved one in the dangerous waters of the North Sea had come true. The knee jerk reaction of the authorities was to make the operators of the type of helicopter – several different companies – ground Super Pumas (except for safety flights where lives were at risk). For a short time, the ban was worldwide. But the Norwegians thought that this incident was 'an isolated case' not connected with other crashes and let them back into the air. In Scotland, too, the aircraft eventually returned to business as usual, though the UK Civil Aviation Authority proposed radical changes to the way helicopters, in this harsh environment, were to be controlled in the future. There were new rules on flying in conditions that made ditching unsafe and work went on to introduce new emergency floating systems and new emergency breathing apparatus. Escape windows were looked at and suggestions made on passenger capacity and seating arrangements. There was also a suggestion of a 'too fat to fly' rule to stop operators from carrying passengers whose body size, including safety and survival equipment, was 'incompatible with push out window emergency exit size'.

Also under review is underwater escape training for oil workers, which is widely regarded as inadequate. That surely, after almost fifty years of rigs working the oilfields, is something that it is hard to forgive. Let us hope that this time the multinational corporations accept their responsibilities to their employees. But there are few grounds for optimism, as some in the industry already favour extending timelines for the introduction of new safety measures. When we talk about the high price of oil, we should remember those who died to keep the pumps running.

14

THE SECRET BATTLE OF MAY ISLAND

Regularly in the summer months from May until October, sturdy little open motor boats sail from the pleasant and popular Fife holiday resorts of Crail and Anstruther (home to what is regularly called in the newspapers the best fish and chip shop in Scotland) and head out to sea towards the cliffs of a large but fairly flat and unspectacular island five miles away in the Firth of Forth. This is May Island, now a nature reserve but a place with a bloody history. The tourists who decant into the peace of the place after forty-five minutes or so on waters that can, at times, be choppy, even in summer, are usually weighed down with picnics, binoculars and cameras and are intent on enjoying the massive selection of seabirds of many breeds – including puffins, guillemots, razor bills, shags, cormorants and terns – that frequent the reserve. Others head first for the remains of the ancient chapel of St Adrian, one of the oldest Christian sites in Scotland, taking in an ancient burial mound on the way. The mound has bones carbon dated at the ninth century and is much visited – and periodically 'dug' – by archaeologists. Some scholars date the remains as even older.

It is pleasant to stroll the paths of the island, enjoying the views of the Lothians and the spectacular Bass Rock to one side and the Fife coast to the other, but it was not always so peaceful. St Adrian was said to have been murdered here by Danish invaders and, indeed, the island is mentioned in *The Orkneyinga Saga* as the site of another bloody raid. But the island has another, more modern secret that comes as a surprise to people who discover what went on here towards the end of the First World War. Here on a dark and misty night, around 100 British Navy men died in one of the most disgraceful episodes in Royal naval history. Some sources put the death toll as higher. A story in *The Guardian* in 2011 put it as high as 270, although most reports suggest that a figure of 104 fatalities was made up by fifty-five dying on submarine *K4*, *K17* losing forty-seven and two from *K14*.

There is probably no definitive answer as, shockingly, the real story of the Battle of May Island, which did not involve any enemy forces, was hushed up at the time and not given the publicity or notoriety that it deserved. The reports that have emerged over time tend to contain inconsistencies and little detail of what really happened.

The main reason given for keeping such a disaster at sea secret for years, or at least not revealing the full horror, was the usual one of not giving succour to the enemy. But it also saved the navy from the embarrassment of the general public hearing a story of colossal incompetence, a story so bizarre that had it appeared in a novel it would have been regarded as absurd and impossible. There was, after the event, a court martial of one officer, and an investigation into what went wrong, but some of the information was not released for more than sixty years, until the death of the last survivor. It is a sad demonstration of the power of the state and the elite who ran the navy at the time that the findings of such an important court martial were not reported contemporaneously in any real detail.

The accident, or series of accidents, for that is what they were, occurred on the night of 31 January to 1 February 1918, during a naval exercise codenamed Operation E.C.1 (using a London postcode hints at the elitism in the ruling class in the navy). Late in 1917, Vice Admiral David Beatty had decided to move two flotillas of K-class subs from Scapa Flow to Rosyth, where it was considered they would be in a better position for North Sea action. By now most in the navy were of the opinion that K stood for 'Katastrophe' or 'Kalamity' and the events off May Island added to the infamous reputation of these submarines. Indeed, Jim Rae of the Scottish branch of the Submariners Association was quoted as saying that those who served in them were known as the suicide club.

Admiral Beatty was well connected and wealthy (the money mainly belonged to his wife, who is reputed to have said to him that if he was upset at the loss of a warship she would buy him another!) and had enjoyed pre-war naval service with the Royal yacht and on various naval ships sauntering from one sunny Mediterranean port to another, in the days when a world war was a distant menace. But he was aggressive and decisive, which is more than can be said of some of his predecessors. He also exhibited upper class sangfroid in spades when the shooting started. During the Battle of Jutland (he also fought naval battles at Heligoland and Dogger Bank), he is reputed to have remarked to his fleet captain: 'there seems to be something wrong with our bloody ships today' after two exploded in half an hour. Quite so, Sir.

On paper, the move south of many ships and subs seemed a good idea tactically. As did a major exercise in the North Sea and further north involving surface vessels, large and small, and submarines – but it was to be a disastrous decision. The size of the exercise was impressive and a reminder that today the Royal Navy has shrunk to the point where it has more captains than ships and that even its newest aircraft carriers are dwarfed by today's giant cruise liners. There is some conflict of opinion in the various archive reports of how many ships were involved. The man in charge was Beatty in his flagship HMS *Queen Elizabeth* and the idea was to practise deployments in the waters around the Orkneys, involving the entire Grand Fleet. This meant that ships and subs based in Roysth in the Firth of Forth had to sail north in convoy to join the exercise. Late in the afternoon of 31 January, around forty vessels left for the north and exercise E.C.1.

There were three battleships, with destroyer escorts, a group of four battlecruisers and their destroyers, two cruisers and two flotillas of K-class subs. As remarked earlier, the only thing the designers of these infernal machines got right was to give them a surface top speed of around 24 knots to enable them to move at the speed of main fleet. The subs were *K3*, *K4*, *K6* and *K7* led by HMS *Fearless* (Captain Charles Little), *K11*, *K12*, *K14*, *K17* and *K22* (formerly *K13* and now back in service after the Gareloch disaster). This group was led by HMS *Ithuriel* (Captain Ernest Leir). Assembled for the journey north, these ships when steaming in a single line made a convoy almost 30 miles long. It was around teatime when this group set sail with two cruisers, *Ithuriel* and *Courageous* at the front followed by the subs of the thirteenth flotilla and then battlecruisers HMS *Australia,* HMS *New Zealand,* HMS *Indomitable* and HMS *Inflexible* and sundry destroyers. Next came the twelfth flotilla of subs and at the rear of this massive array of naval power, the battleships.

It would have been an impressive sight if visible from the shore, which is unlikely, as the night was deeply dark and with the drifting mists that so bedevil navigation in these waters. This was not good weather for such a number of ships to be in close proximity in the days before radar and GPS. There was, of course, another threat – German U-boats, and in fact there had been rumours of one operating in the area before the Rosyth boats headed out. This meant there was radio silence between the ships and subs, and only the stern light of the vessel in front was there to guide the helmsmen. And even these lights had been dimmed because of the fear of U-boat attack. Also the lights were shaded so that they were prevented from being seen more than one compass point from the centre line of the vessel. This made the 'follow the leader' plan more dangerous. But no enemy hand played a direct part in the Battle of May Island, a title given to the episode in black humour rather than reflecting reality.

If a battle it wasn't, there was no doubt that it was a disaster waiting to happen. It is always the unexpected that causes things to go wrong, and so it was with operation E.C.1. The trigger of what was to become chaos was simple. The convoy was passing May Island and increasing speed when, just as the thirteenth sub flotilla passed the island, lights of other vessels were spotted approaching the subs. This is now thought to have been the lights of minesweeping naval trawlers. You would, of course, have thought the convoy would have known the position of other navy vessels. Apparently not. The subs were turned sharply to port to avoid the mystery vessels. Then came another unexpected development – *K14*'s helm jammed and she veered out of position. *K14* and the boat behind her, *K12*, were forced to turn on their navigation lights in an attempt to see what was going on. The dodgy helm was eventually freed and the sub managed to get back in line. But worse was to come.

The next sub in line was our old friend *K13*, now in its new life as *K22*. The number change had done nothing for her luck though, and as the mist swirled she was in trouble. Her crew lost sight of the vessels around and she veered out of line and collided with *K14*. The rest of the fleet was continuing out to sea unaware of what had happened in their wake.

The two damaged subs had completely stopped and were drifting helplessly in the darkness. Threat from U-boats or not, the radio silence was broken. And the message going out over the airwaves was grim: *K22* told the cruiser leading the flotilla, in code, that despite damage they thought they could reach port. Not so for the *K14*. The damage to her was such that she was sinking fast. Ships were still steaming around at high speed in darkness and confusion. The mist and darkness was broken into by occasional flare lights shining down on a scene of increasing mayhem.

Next up was the second battlecruiser squadron, which largely managed to pass the island and miss the two damaged subs, but it was only going to get worse for *K22*, which was suddenly smashed into by the following ironically named battlecruiser, HMS *Inflexible*. This was no glancing blow – the force of the collision bent the first 30 feet of *K22*'s bows at right angles to the rest of the vessel. Ironically, the disaster in this submarine's previous existence as *K13* had killed those in the stern: now the bow area was a mangled wreck with ballast and fuel tanks destroyed. Not surprisingly, the sub settled into the water and only the conning tower showed above the waves.

But the nightmare for the rest of the convoy was far from over. On board the *Ithuriel*, the coded messages on the first collision of the subs had been decoded and the captain turned back and steamed to the rescue. This would not have happened in a real sea battle situation rather than during war games. The subs trailing *Ithuriel* also turned to follow her, crossing the path of the second battle squadron in the process. It was becoming like a hideous naval version of dodgem cars with ships and subs frantically altering course to avoid each other in the dark and mist. Somehow, all the emergency alterations of course managed to avoid further collisions. At least for the moment, but when the thirteenth flotilla got back into the May Island vicinity, they encountered the twelfth flotilla outbound. Another collision was inevitable and HMS *Fearless* steamed into *K17*, causing her to sink in minutes. Fortunately, however, many of the crew managed to jump overboard.

Fearless was now powerless and in the way of her following subs. There were near misses and contacts. HMS *Australia*, a battlecruiser, had a near miss with *K12*, forcing her onto a collision path with *K6*. This sub desperately took action to avoid *K12* but instead hit *K4*. The impact of this collision was such that *K4* was almost cut in half. What it must have been like for officers and crews of the ships involved in this nightmare nautical dance of death is almost

190

beyond imagination. Not surprisingly, what was left of *K4* sank, taking all of her crew to the deep. In the process of sinking, *K4* was also hit by *K7*. It is almost unbelievable that in the midst of all this, three battleships and their destroyers passed through the area unaware of what was going on. With this came some of the most horrific scenes of the whole black episode as the survivors of *K17*, struggling in the water, were cut down in the dark by the destroyers. Only nine of the fifty-six men on this sub survived, with one dying of his injuries shortly after being plucked from the water.

All this is said to have happened in seventy-five minutes of hell – *K17* and *K4* sunk, *K6*, *K7*, *K14*, *K22* and HMS *Fearless* damaged. This book is peppered with the stories of cairns, statues, plaques and the like erected in the memory of men and women who died at sea. In the case of the victims of the Battle of May Island, it took eighty-four years before a cairn was placed at Anstruther harbour with May Island looming large out on the waters of the Firth in the distance. The wording on the cairn does not discuss the cause of the disaster, though relatives of those who died at least have some consolation in that the Submariners Association holds a commemorative service there each year.

This was one of the worst-ever naval disasters in our waters and something which surely could never be repeated. A mix of bad planning, bad judgement and bad luck left a total of 104 men dead and others injured. With the chaos that happened, perhaps the only crumb of comfort is that even more lives were not lost in this tragic episode.

15

WITCHES ON BROOMSTICKS
AND BLACK FRIDAY

One of the pleasures of a coastal holiday in Scotland is a stroll round any of the hundreds of harbours that serve as a base for the remaining fisher folk who work the waters for a living. The seagulls wheel and shriek, the smell of fresh fish lingers and the sunshine can sparkle on the glistening fish scales that encrust the hard-working vessels. In the summer, it is a scene of peace and tranquillity. In the winter, it is a different story, no more so than on the east coast.

From the far north-east down to the Scottish borders, the North Sea, winter spells danger. It has been like this for hundreds of years. As far back as 1577, the historical records tell of massive loss of life at the fishing. In that year, it is said that 1,000 boats were wrecked off the coast of Dunbar in the south-east. Here, the fishermen ignored the tradition adhered to in most other areas of Scotland, of not putting to sea on a Sunday. Working on the Sabbath was something the God-fearing in the community did not approve of and many people of the church were of the opinion that no good would come of it. Ministers thumped their Bibles, drew their black robes around them and harangued the congregations on the dangers of such lack of respect for the Sabbath. Feelings ran so high that the Dunbar men were known as 'ungodly fishers who went to sea while godly men were journeying to church'. A drawing of the time showed fishing boats in a storm, with witches on broomsticks flying above them. And, indeed, the local minister, one Andrew Simpson, had warned of disasters ahead if this sort of behaviour was not given up. One ancient tome gives some detail and from it God seems to have been, according to Simpson, a vengeful deity bound on creating widows and orphans.

In a book published in 1830, the author James Miller quotes a Kirk session record: 'Mr Simpson, minister of Dalkeith, son to Mr Andrew Simpson minister of Dunbar, hath these words: "a fearful judgement of God fell furth at Dunbar about the year of God 1577. I was an eyewitness. My father Andrew Simpson, of good memory, being minister thereof, going to the church, saw a thousand boats setting their nets on the Sabbath day. He wept and feared God would not suffer such contempt – at midnight, when they went forth to draw their nets, the wind arose so fearfully, that it drowned eight score and ten boats so that there was reckoned in the coast side fourteen score of widows."

Maybe the habits of the fishermen thereabouts contributed to the first of three major fishing disasters to blight the area, but I doubt it. More likely, the most important factor in what became known as 'The Legend of the Lost Drave' was the design of the boats. Or our old favourite: ignored weather warnings. In these days, the fishing boats were small and open and unsuitable for the North Sea, except in relatively calm weather. It took until the mid-nineteenth century for bigger and fully decked boats to be built. And

193

for a time traditionalists resisted the new designs. Some thought it was safer to be deep down in an open boat rather than on a deck exposed to the wave and weather. In fact, it was late in the twentieth century, in the era of steel hulled boats, before guardrails and other safety devices appeared. Wooden decked boats had only a foot or so of boarding to stop an unwary fisherman being swept into the sea. On such boats even a slight slip or a foot tangled momentarily in a loose rope end could have a fatal ending. And though an improvement, the lack of railings on new boats and the heavy boots and thick woollen gear worn by the crews made it almost certain that anyone washed overboard would drown quickly. No health and safety, no rafts, no life jackets, no flares – the death toll was high, the real price paid for putting fresh fish in the diets of thousands.

The loss of life, the Dunbar disaster apart, was mostly in dribs and drabs, a man lost here and another there. It was a fact of life at sea. But there was another exception to this rule, in 1848, when for once it was a summer storm that did the damage. In August of that year it is said that in the north-east 124 boats went down and 100 fishermen drowned. Harbours in these days were not as safe as now and many of the casualties were the results of vessels trying to make the shelter of the crude breakwaters around the little bays from which the fishermen had set out. An inquiry was set up and Captain John Washington was charged with producing a report on what went on. His main conclusion was that decked boats would be safer and that harbours used by the fishermen needed improving. Not a surprising verdict.

These early fishing disasters were a hint of what was to come and, in 1881, what seems, with hindsight, to be the inevitable happened on Black Friday – the day of the tragic

Eyemouth fishing disaster, which claimed 129 from that town alone. Religion played a role here as well as in the earlier incidents. The most important retelling of the tale comes from an Eyemouth man, Peter Aitchison, in his book *Black Friday*, originally published as *Children of the Sea*. Aitchison, a historian and BBC reporter, has uncovered great detail of this horrific event. The 'back story', as newspaper folk call it, stretches to the early nineteenth century. The biblical concept of worshippers giving a tithe of 10 per cent of their earnings to the church was fully imposed on the east coast and the east coast fishermen, though the policy was far from consistent in other areas of the country and in other occupations such as farming.

Aitcheson remarks that not surprisingly the fishermen resented what was going on and even that 'they hated the kirk'. Even the local laird thought the imposition of this fish tax was a bad thing. Some of the men would rather give their catch to French boats lying offshore than land it in Scotland. The row was a serious one, so serious that far off Whitehall and the Treasury insisted that the 10 per cent tithe was claimed. The inconsistency in this edict did not seem to worry the mandarins in London, then as now, oblivious to the realities of life beyond the capital. Peter Aitchison puts all this into context by pointing out that in 1845, 10 per cent of the annual catch was the more than substantial sum of £4,000. Remember that this was more than 150 years ago.

Away from this religious row, another problem was simmering in the background. Even all these years ago, it was accepted that the harbour at Eyemouth needed to be deepened and more protection provided against the North Sea swells. But Eyemouth had a rival for the money needed for this scheme – Peterhead, much further up the east coast.

And Peterhead got the money in a controversial political decision. At that time, the harbour problem was not local to towns south of the Tay, though it was indeed a difficulty in such places. Apart from the fishing disasters, there had been numerous shipwrecks on the east coast involving coasters, whalers bound for far distant waters and ships trading with the continent. The weather was unpredictable, with even some immense summer storms as previously mentioned. North of Newcastle there was nothing that could be called 'a harbour of refuge', a safe place for vessels, including naval ships, seeking shelter from storms.

The festering row between kirk and fishermen undoubtedly played a role in the decision to construct the huge new harbour in Peterhead rather than Eyemouth, as many wanted. Though it has to be said there were other good reasons to favour Peterhead. However, the government felt no pressure to help the Eyemouth men, who were seen as troublesome rebels who burned tax demands and under the leadership of William Spiers, called the Kingfisher, refused orders to appear in court. Spiers, incidentally, was a distant relative of Peter Aitchison.

But Peterhead did have other practical advantages. Its existing 'lagoon' was large and when protected by huge new breakwaters – the largest in the world at the time – it was safe for even the largest sailing vessels and the new breed of steam-powered trawlers and coasters, and navy ships as well. Peterhead had it all: the best granite in the world, a natural harbour suited to development and labour was to be no problem because the Scottish government was to build a new prison overlooking the harbour. In the south, there was the example of Dover harbour constructed by convict labour. So in the late 1880s work began, including a pioneering 'nationalised' railway to transport prisoners to the quarries to hew the huge stone blocks needed. The same little line then transported the stone to the harbour site, where other prisoners dressed it and dropped it into place under the guidance of civilian engineers and Admiralty men. It took until after the Second World War to complete, but the success of this idea is evident when on a winter day you stand and look out to the huge rollers smashing themselves harmlessly onto the Aberdeen granite as ships lie peacefully in the inner harbour. The law of unintended consequences came into play in Peterhead too – what a stroke of luck that when the liquid gold under the North Sea was discovered there was the perfect onshore oil industry base to take pressure off nearby Aberdeen.

All this was, of course, no consolation to Eyemouth, who had missed out on the big prize and where the effects of the war over the tithe lingered on. As in any war, rumours abounded. One rumour in the town was that gunships were assembling offshore and even that cavalry were gathering on the border for a sortie against the rebels. It was, of course, just rumours, but the local minister had his windows smashed time after time for his determination to collect the hated tithe. Eventually, in the tradition of gang-blighted Glasgow housing schemes, the manse became an ugly boarded-up building. The situation was getting out of control and in 1861 the legal authorities stepped in with a compromise involving the fishermen buying out the kirk tax for £2,000. It was not satisfactory, as the fishermen had to borrow the money and it took years to pay it back. This had a direct influence on the 1881 disaster. Years of struggling to make every penny they could meant that the Eyemouth men and those from surrounding villages were used to sailing to work in conditions where others would stay in the safety of a harbour. They needed the money. One advantage was that with the war, with the kirk suspended, Whitehall gave permission for an improved harbour, though not one on the scale of Peterhead. Ironically, this was just a few weeks before the fleet sailed into disaster.

Earlier I mentioned the pleasure of wandering round harbours 'looking at the boats' with their names often redolent of family or friends, west coast or east coast you often find the same names. The fleet that sailed from Eyemouth on the calm and sunny morning of Friday, 14 October 1881 included many of the old favourites – *Guiding Star, Invincible, Stormy Petrel, Concord* and *Fisher Lass*. The preparation for the voyage – baiting the hooks of the many long lines with thousands of mussels and whelks – took place without anyone paying too much attention to the fact that the barometer was as low as it had ever been seen in the fishing town. No attention was paid either to the closeness of the date to Friday the thirteenth. The years of struggle maximising the catch to pay the debts had hardened skippers and crews to take a chance with the weather.

It was only an hour or two before the storm struck with little warning. The sails were set, those long, long lines ready for the water. With the sun setting, nineteen boats had been sunk and nearly 200 men had been killed. Most of the fishermen were from Eyemouth (129) but some were from nearby villages such as Burnmouth, St Abbs, Coldingham Shore and Cove. Others were from Musselburgh's Fisherrow and Newhaven. The stark facts disguise the full horror. Like the nightmare in Stornoway harbour years later, when the *Iolaire* hit the Beasts of Holm, many families watched helplessly as their loved ones perished. Wives, mothers, children were at the still inadequate harbour to witness the horror. Some were in hysterics. Seventy widows and around 300 children were left in poverty and grief. It took around 100 years for the population of the Berwickshire village to reach the level it had been at in 1881. The fact that so many men and so much of the fleet had been lost, meant that any grandiose plans for a harbour of refuge were completely lost. Real improvements to the harbour had to wait many decades.

The human consequences were catastrophic. Many women – who often worked in the 'family business' baiting the long lines to catch haddock and herring – lost husbands, brothers and sons. Many wept onshore as they heard the cries for help. Those on the few boats that did survive lost brothers and fathers. The crews who did not die out at sea or attempting the dangerous rocky entrance to the old harbour did so by heading out to sea to ride out the storm rather than flee for the apparent safety of the shore. Or they took quick decisions to head for harbours south of the town. One vessel that rode out the storm did not return until two days later and the skipper was so tired that he had to be carried ashore, unable to stand. This poor man then had to attend the funeral of his son, who had died on another boat.

Now in the twenty-first century, such an unprecedented disaster would have resulted in social workers, psychologists and others descending in flocks to the town to help with the grief – and the feeding and clothing of the bereaved. Nothing could erase the pain, but society would show compassion. Maybe some of the modern embodiments of such community care were missing, but Scotland responded with great generosity and common sense to what had happened. This was probably the worst fishing disaster in modern

British history. Money flowed from all over the country and more than £50,000 was collected, an immense sum for those days. The Disaster Fund allowed widows to get five shillings a week and half a crown for each child who attended school. Unborn children were also to be looked after. To the great credit of Scotland and the people of Eyemouth, all 260 fatherless children were adopted and stayed in the town. The toll on the people in the years after was horrendous: widows died heartbroken, men turned to the bottle or simply succumbed to depression, and others died of overwork looking after the families of the fleet.

Today in Eyemouth harbour, there is a memorial remembering the disaster. Sadly it is just one of too many around the headlands, cliff tops and harbours on storm lashed islands, and the mainland, all of which are a poignant reminder of the relentless power of Scotland's cruel sea to take life. These memorials, some large and impressive, some unobtrusive cairns, others simple plaques on a harbour wall, are a moving testimony to the memory of those who died.

Scotland will not forget them.

SELECTED SOURCES AND
SUGGESTED FURTHER READING

Newspapers and magazines:
Aviation Weekly & Space Technology
Campbeltown Courier
Clydesite.co.uk
Daily Record
Daily Telegraph
Dundee Evening Telegraph
Forargyll.com
Guardian, The
Herald, The
Hull Daily News
Kintyre Magazine, The
Oban Times
Press and Journal
Shetland Times, The
Scots Magazine, The
Scotsman, The
Stornoway Gazette

Books:

Aitchison, Peter. *Black Friday: The Eyemouth Disaster of 1881* (Birlinn).

Courtney, Charles. *Unlocking Adventure* (Hale).

Crawford, Ian and Moir, Peter. *Argyll Shipwrecks* (Moir Crawford).

Gillies, Freddie. *The Viking Isle* (Ardminish Press).

——*Silver from the Sea* (Ardminish Press).

MacLeod, John. *When I Heard the Bell: The Loss of the Iolaire* (Birlinn).

MacVicar, Angus. *Rescue Call* (Littlehampton Book Service Ltd).

Martin, Angus. *The Ring-net Fishermen* (John Donald Publishers).

McKay, Sinclair. *The Secret Life of Bletchley Park: The History of the Wartime Codebreaking Centre by the Men and Women Who Were There* (Aurum Press Ltd).

Norman, Nelson. *In Search of a Penguin's Egg* (AuthorHouse).

——*In Search of Remote Health Care* (The Lumphanan Press).

Ralston, Tommy. *To the Edge: Confessions of a Lifeboat Coxswain* (Scottish Cultural Press).

——*Captains and Commanders: Confessions of a Scottish West Coast Fisherman* (Mallaig Heritage Centre).

——*Son of a Gun* (Ardminish Press).

Steele, John and Noreen. *The Secrets of HMS Dasher* (Argyll Publishing).

——*The American Connection to the Sinking of HMS Dasher* (North Shore Publishing).

——*They Were Never Told: Tragedy of HMS Dasher* (Argyll Publishing).

INDEX